EQUIPPED TO LOVE

EQUIPPED TO LOVE

Idolatry-Free Relationships

Norm Wakefield

The Spirit of

Elijah

MINISTRIES

a non-profit corporation

Bulverde, Texas

Equipped To Love:
Idolatry-Free Relationships

Published by Spirit of Elijah Ministries
        30063 US Highway 281N, PMB 801
        Bulverde, Texas 78163

Cover design: Brian Dreiling

First printing: 1999
Second printing: 2001

Printed in the United States of America

ISBN 1-892754-00-2

Library of Congress
Catalog Card Number: 98-96449

*To Alma, my faithful and beloved
wife--my friend, encourager,
and soul-mate*

CONTENTS

Preface

It could well be argued that the one character quality that the church should demonstrate most is love. A pastor often deals with people who want to love but don't know how or understand why they seem powerless to love. That need inspired me to write this book.

I know there are many books available telling Christians that we ought to love, but I've found few if any that get into the nuts and bolts of why we can't love or how we can love. Although loving can't be reduced to the mere application of knowledge and the observance of a set of guidelines, I am encouraged by the responses to the message of this book. I believe that God will use the insights from the Scriptures to equip you to love.

I'm sure there are many resources I could have recommended to you in this endeavor, but I've purposely limited them to a few (I'm almost embarrassed by the brevity of the endnotes page in the back). Specifically, I've trusted in the wisdom and insight from the Scriptures and have relied upon them as the curriculum for equipping you to love.

I've also written *Equipped to Love* because I needed it! I've heard someone say that preachers preach about what they need to apply in their own lives. Such is the case with me! I so appreciate my wife, Alma, and my children: Abby, Alyssa, Micah, and Amanda, who are having to endure my learning time. I wish I had been equipped to love before I became a husband and father, but I wasn't. And perhaps you weren't, either.

I've written this book for husbands who want to know how to love their wives, for wives who desire to love their husbands, for parents who long to love their children with Jesus' love, for children and teens who struggle to love their brothers, sisters, and parents, and for the people of God who want to love Him more.

The assault on marriage and family from our humanistic and hedonistic society also has inspired me to write. Marriages suffer tremendously because many pre-marriage and marriage relationships were built on a foundation of idolatry. Consequently, those marriages are in shambles today. The divorce rate in the church is almost as high as in secular society. If you're one whose marriage is in jeopardy, and you feel that love has disappeared in your relationship, then I'm grateful to God that He's brought this book your way. You're one of the reasons this book exists! It's never too late to become equipped to love.

In the last two years, two of my daughters have married. What a blessing it is to see their marriages begin with a foundation on the love of Jesus Christ. I'm sure you see the value of preparing your children to enter into marriage equipped to love. I hope one of the main uses of this book will be in the establishment of firm foundations for new marriages.

Regardless of your age, gender, or marriage condition, I don't think you'll be disappointed over the time you spend reading *Equipped to Love*. These truths and insights have been used by God to save marriages, transform relationships, and inspire a greater love for God.

I am grateful to God for what He has given through His Word, His Son, Jesus Christ, and by His Spirit. Also I would like to take this opportunity to mention several people who have contributed directly or indirectly to this book.

First, I want to express my deep gratitude to the members of Coast Community Church in Fountain Valley, California, for their tremendous sacrificial support and encouragement. Their willingness to provide the time, the financial support for my family, and the inspiration for this book can only be attributed to God's gracious work in their hearts and is a demonstration of His love to me.

Second, I appreciate Jerry White, Jr., for his invaluable Christ-centered critique and insights. Not only has he influenced the book with his comments, but his example of love through the years has made an indelible impression on my life.

Finally, God has made my family such an encouragement to me. Next to Jesus, it has primarily been through them and with them that God is teaching and equipping me to love.

Introduction

LOVE --a word usually stripped of its power. We love our cars, houses, jobs, sports, hobbies, and a million other things. But what do most people mean when they say they love their cars? Do they love cars like they love people? All too often, the answer is, "Yes." When we confuse the way we love things with the way we love God and people, we find ourselves frustrated and failing.

Do you struggle to love God? If you've grown up attending church, you know that you're supposed to love God. The apostle Paul wrote, "If anyone does not love the Lord, let him be accursed" (1 Corinthians 16:22). That verse has a sobering effect on me. The fear of not loving God enough has haunted me more times than I can count. I know I don't love God as I ought. His mercies, His Word, His forgiveness, His watchful care over me, His gifts, His intercession on my behalf, His death and resurrection ought to evoke a deep and consistent love, but sometimes my love is cold. In fact, frequently I detect within myself attitudes toward God that I know are wrong.

For instance, just after my spiritual new birth at age 29, I discovered a bitterness toward God that was affecting my relationship with Him. It was a bitterness springing from my frustration with God's timing in revealing Himself to me. I didn't like it that God let me struggle through seventeen years of tiresome, fruitless striving to make myself acceptable to God and my own conscience. I didn't understand God's love or know how to love. Although now I'm at peace with

God's timing, I can't help but wish a book such as this had come into my hands then.

Are there some people who tax you to the limit of your ability to love? Quite often, the people we want to love the most are the ones with whom we have the most difficulty. Perhaps you can relate to the couple I counseled who were struggling to persevere in a marriage characterized by a love/hate relationship. They said they loved each other, yet they often couldn't stand each other. They pushed each other's buttons at the drop of a hat. Wouldn't you like to know why you have difficulty loving your wife, husband, child, brother, sister, or work associate? Even more, don't you want to glorify God by loving them with His love?

If you think that you can't love, that you suffer from a severe, incurable case of self-centeredness, that you need to be motivated to try harder to love, you'll be pleased to discover the answer doesn't lie in more effort on your part. If you desire to grow in your love for God and others, you'll be encouraged by learning God's purposes for relationships. Gaining insight into what God is doing in you as He brings difficult people and circumstances into your life will produce wisdom and hope. You'll also discover how God works through people and circumstances to lead you to Himself and to a deeper experience of His love flowing through you.

The purpose of this book is to equip you to recognize deceptive, unloving attitudes and actions, then direct you to the Source of love. You'll learn to:

♦ Distinguish between God's kind of love and the world's kind of love.
♦ Remove a destructive attitude of idolatry with regard to God, others, and circumstances.
♦ Recognize the characteristics of the spirit of idolatry.
♦ Love as God loves.

The kind of love of which I will be writing is represented by the Greek word, *agape*. This kind of love transcends all kinds of love and provides the basis for both brotherly (phileo) love and physical (eros) love. We want to mature to the point that love becomes the motivation in all our relationships. We read in the Scriptures that God's Word searches and exposes the hidden, destructive motives of our hearts.

> For the word of God is living and active and sharper than any two-edged sword, and piercing as far as the division of soul and spirit, of both joints and marrow, and able to judge the thoughts and intentions of the heart. And there is no creature hidden from His sight, but all things are open and laid bare to the eyes of Him with whom we have to do (Hebrews 4:12-13).

This is necessary if our love is to be refined and matured. I believe the insights from God's Word will be powerful and life-changing.

The desire and the burden of my heart is to see God produce, through Christian families, children who not only are educated, skilled, and trained, but children who love. I also wish to implant a wonderful vision in parents' minds. Think of the impact of a generation of young adults who have been influenced by the power of the love in their homes to the point of being able to influence the next generation.

Parenting children and successfully rearing them to love the Lord, to be responsible and skilled, and to contribute to the kingdom of God involves many factors. We're concerned about the education factor, the health factor, the practical skills factor, the spiritual factor, the social factor, and the factor of character.

Of all these factors in the parenting equation, the most important factor according to God's Word is the love factor. The apostle Paul put it succinctly when he placed a low value on education without love. He wrote to the Corinthians, "And if I have the gift of prophecy, and know all mysteries and all knowledge; and if I have all faith, so as to remove mountains, but do not have love, I am nothing" (I Corinthians 13:2).

What is the love factor in your life? In your home? Would you like to increase this aspect of your home life and relationships? I hope so. What wonderful freedom lies before you. May God equip you to love.

"Heavenly Father, Source of Love, enable me to simply and clearly share the hindrances to love which You've revealed in Your Word. May Your Spirit rest upon this one who writes and those who read. Anoint us with the power to love. Grant us grace to understand the truths presented and apply them to our relationships. And we'll thank You and give You all the glory. Amen."

PART ONE

Lessons
About Love

Chapter 1

WHICH KIND OF LOVE?

Distinguish between God's kind of love and the world's kind of love.

S ince the word "love" is used so frequently, I've fround it helpful to make a clear distinction between the world's kind of love
and God's kind of love. They are poles apart.

The World's Kind of Love

The world's kind of love focuses on getting and using. The
apostle John described it in his first letter.

> Do not love the world, nor the things in the world. If anyone
> loves the world, the love of the Father is not in him. For all
> that is in the world, the lust of the flesh and the lust of the
> eyes and the boastful pride of life, is not from the Father, but
> is from the world (I John 2:15-16).

When John spoke of the world, he alluded to those who do not
belong to Jesus. In speaking to His disciples about the gift of the Holy
Spirit, Jesus distinguished His own from those of the world.

> And I will ask the Father, and He will give you another Helper,
> that He may be with you forever; that is the Spirit of truth,

whom the world cannot receive because it does not behold Him or know Him, but you know Him because He abides in you, and will be in you (John 14:16-17).

Since the *world cannot receive the Holy Spirit*, there's no way the world's kind of love is like God's kind of love. Further in the same discourse, Jesus cited a difference between the world's mindset and the mindset of those who were His. *We see that the world loves itself and hates Jesus and His people.*

If the world hates you, you know that it has hated Me before it hated you. If you were of the world, the world would love its own; but because you are not of the world, but I chose you out of the world, therefore the world hates you (John 15:18-19).

Perhaps the world's kind of love may best be described by what the apostle John wrote in his first epistle. He wrote that the love of the world may be summarized as "the lust of the flesh and the lust of the eyes and the boastful pride of life" (1 John 2:16).

The world values things and people based upon their usability. Perhaps you've noticed when they use the word "love" as a verb, they mean that the object of their love gives them something they want. For instance, when someone of the world states, "I love my car," he probably has in mind the benefit the car brings to his life, either through its ability to enhance his image or through its problem-free service. If someone in the world had an old clunker like mine, he probably wouldn't speak so affectionately. It doesn't give anything but an opportunity to trust God!

When a worldling says he loves his wife, he probably means that she does for him what he wants her to do most of the time and when he wants her to do it. As long as she makes him happy and comfortable, she has value to him which he expresses with the term "love."

On the flip side of the coin, someone might use the opposite term of hate for those objects which don't make his life easier. A wife may say she hates her husband or her children because they don't do things her way in her time. Usually this hatred develops over a period of time, but the concept is clear: *The world's kind of love centers on getting and using.*

God's Kind of Love

In stark contrast, *God's kind of love focuses on giving and serving.* My wife and I are being taught this lesson by God through Amanda, our daughter with Down's Syndrome. We were totally surprised by Amanda's condition when she arrived. It was life-changing immediately for many reasons, but the first was the exposure of the world's kind of love in our thinking towards her and the rest of our children. We had specific prayer requests entered in our prayer notebooks, and Amanda was not the answer to *those* prayers!

Upon her arrival, our selfish motives behind our prayers were hung out naked on the cross. Faced with our disappointment and inability to find any use or selfish benefit from her existence, we were shaken to the core. We wanted a child from whom we could get something--a little girl we could use to get glory for ourselves and who wouldn't be a bother. Of course, we desired that she be the sort of person others would "love" also--someone to whom they would be attracted because of what she could offer them.

I'm ashamed to admit it, but before Amanda was born, we expected her value to consist of her capacity to be used and to contribute to our lives. Now I see that God loved us enough to reveal how warped our ideas were of His love, and I'm glad He did! It opened up to us a new appreciation and understanding of the love of God. This came as He revealed how I was in a similar condition to Amanda in my relationship to Him--useless, but in need of love.

Our Value to God

As a sinner, I was of no use to Jesus Christ except as an object who drew out of Him the love of His Father. The verses in Romans 3:10-12 took on new meaning. "There is none righteous, not even one; there is none who understands, there is none who seeks for God; all have turned aside, *together they have become useless*; there is none who does good, there is not even one." That's us, humans. We're drastically deformed and worse than spiritually retarded!

My sinfulness offers the occasion for God, the Father, to demonstrate His kind of love--a pure, giving love. When Jesus says, "I love

21

you," He means that I am of value because of what I draw out of Him--the love of His Father. In the same way, I saw that to love Amanda, I was going to have to make a distinction between the world's kind of love and God's kind of love. From the world's viewpoint, I had no reason to love Amanda. But by the grace of God revealed in the gospel, love took on a new meaning. Have you ever thought that the great value of the ones whom you have trouble loving is that they cause you to go to your heavenly Father? Amanda's and everyone's value comes from their ability to draw out what God puts in--His kind of love--thus bringing glory to God.

God gives great freedom when we realize that *people and situations offer opportunities for God to demonstrate the reality of our relationship to Him*. He gives them for the purpose of testing and revealing who His children are. As He loves through us, we realize that we are loved by God. People and situations are God-given for the purpose of testing and revealing the children of God, the objects of God's love. The Amandas in life, therefore, cause us to realize the power of sin and the power of love. If we only have the world's kind of love within us, sin's powerful, selfish grip on our hearts will be evident in our inability to love. But if Jesus dwells within us, we may experience His powerful love flowing through us. In both cases, they're God's instruments, drawing out what fills our hearts.

I'll never forget what my good friend and mentor, Jerry White, said: "Every relationship is an opportunity to love, and every situation is an opportunity to trust." Oswald Chambers wrote, "A man's disposition on the inside, i.e., what he possesses in his personality, determines what he is tempted by on the outside. The temptation fits the nature of the one tempted, and reveals the possibilities of the nature. Every man has the setting of his own temptation, and the temptation will come along the line of the ruling disposition."[1] God knows just what we need in order to expose the disposition of worldly love and lead us into repentance and the infilling and outpouring of His love.

The chart below contrasts the two kinds of love. If we only know of the world's love, we will only be happy with the "user-friendlies" in life. Our relationships will show it. We'll find ourselves jealously seeking to control everything and everyone we deem useful. We may often deal with anger and jealousy, and we may be offended easily.

But if we know the love of Christ, a giving kind of love flows out of us as we live out of Christ's fullness. It's a kind of love which provides a basis for unity. Wanting the best for everyone and deferring self for others, we are able to serve others without jealousy or offense. Since it flows out of a vital union with Jesus Christ, all the glory goes to God. As John wrote,

> Beloved, let us love one another, for love is from God; and everyone who loves is born of God and knows God. The one who does not love does not know God, for God is love (I John 4:7-8).

Ponder these distinctives

World's Kind of Love	vs	God's Kind of Love
Source: Self-love		Source: God in Jesus Christ
Motivation: To get		Motivation: To give
Purpose: To use		Purpose: To be used
Exalts man		Exalts God
Requires no faith; natural		Requires faith; spiritual
Value determined by usability of the object/person		Value determined by the opportunity provided to show Jesus' love
Selfish in nature		Focuses on others
Controlling; manipulating		Yielding; serving
Jealous		Not jealous
Fails		Doesn't fail
Hates suffering		Endures suffering
Based on temporal values		Based on eternal values
No power to unify		Perfect bond of unity
Based on feelings		Based on fact
Can be angered and offended		Cannot be angered or offended
Driven by emptiness		Driven by fullness

Perhaps here's a new thought. The greater one's uselessness, inability, or stubbornness, the greater potential there is for you to experience God's love. Is there anyone you know you ought to love, but have found it difficult to do so? Could it be that the world's philosophy of love has found a home in your thinking? If you notice it, you perhaps are standing at the threshold of experiencing God's love in a powerful way.

When God revealed this thought to me, I asked the Lord to show the relationships that kind of thinking had destroyed or damaged so that I could ask Him for a thorough repentance and demonstrate His love for His glory. I enjoyed more freedom than ever before and saw my ability to love grow as I had a change of mind and heart about those relationships.

Many others have given the same testimony. One woman informed me that the realization of her worldly love for her husband saved her marriage. Moms, frustrated with their children because they were not user-friendly, have expressed the joy of renewed and healed relationships. Husbands have gained a new vision for loving their wives as they see the difference between the world's kind of love and God's kind of love.

Can you think of a relationship with which you are presently struggling? Are you frustrated over something that you are not *getting* from that person that you feel you deserve? Do they inconvenience *you*? If they were to do things your way in your time, would you feel like you *love* them more?

Please take some time to let God examine your heart through this first insight about love. He may bring numerous relationships to mind which have been based entirely on the use you could make of them. If so, there's no need to feel overwhelmed or discouraged with what you see about yourself. Instead, be encouraged: God works in mysterious ways, His wonders to perform! Your sinfulness and lack of love have been the occasion for Jesus Christ to demonstrate the love of His Father toward you.

> But God demonstrates His own love toward us, in that while
> we were yet sinners, Christ died for us (Romans 5:8).

I encourage you to receive His love and forgiveness as you confess to God each relationship which has been damaged by the world's kind of love. You are experiencing the benefits of understanding God's way to loving relationships. Ask Him to reveal more as we look further into Jesus' love.

Chapter 2

IDOLATRY-FREE
RELATIONSHIPS

**Learn the Love Principle:
You can't love anyone you idolize.**

According to the Scriptures, the spirit of idolatry lies at the heart of every sin. God's first commandment in the Ten Commandments dealt with the iniquity of idolatry. The prophet Samuel informed King Saul that insubordination and rebellion are as idolatry (I Samuel 15:23). The apostle Paul encouraged the Colossians to consider themselves dead to immorality, impurity, passion, evil desire, and greed, which amount to idolatry (Colossians 3:5). We could say that idolatry embodies everything that is antichrist.

Whenever someone looks to anything or anyone other than God as the source of all things, he commits the sin of idolatry. This may sound strange, but it's true. Here is a good definition of idolatry: looking to any person, object, or idea to supply what only God can supply. For instance, when a husband looks to his wife to make him happy, he idolizes her. If a child looks to himself for the ability to please his parents, he idolizes himself. A wife might idolize her children by expecting them to make her significant. This may be contrasted with the idea of "looking to" God as the supplier of our needs. It might be helpful to realize that when we look to God for all things, we are worshiping God.

We can easily see how the sins mentioned in Colossians 3 constitute idolatry, but when the spirit of idolatry masquerades as light or kindness, it displays its most devilish characteristic. Just as Satan often portrays himself as an angel or messenger of light, this diabolical spirit often pawns itself off as love, in the worldly sense. So if someone doesn't distinguish between the world's kind of love and God's kind of love, he can be duped into the opinion that he is loving when in fact he is using someone for selfish interest.

That's why it's so important to learn to recognize the spirit of idolatry. It slithers its way into relationships from the very seed of our human nature. At the heart of Satan's temptation of Adam and Eve lies idolatry and self-will. He tempts us to ignore God's Word and will, to listen to him, and to enthrone our own wills. With such bait, he lured the parents of the human race away from looking to God alone as the source of power, wisdom, and happiness. From the time Satan's seed was planted and bore fruit in Adam and Eve, idolatry has hindered relationships.

Typically when we hear the word "idolatry," our minds conjure up a prehistoric man chiseling a block of stone. Many think of it as an Old Testament sin that modern man has outgrown. But have we really outgrown it, or have we merely sophisticated it?

While meditating on Galatians 5:14, I was struck with the fact that the whole Law is fulfilled in one word: love. It reads, "For the whole Law is fulfilled in one word, in the statement, 'You shall love your neighbor as yourself.'" That prompted me to meditate on the Ten Commandments to see how each one relates to love. What I discovered in the first commandment is vital to being equipped to love--insight into the characteristics of the spirit of idolatry.

Love can only take place where a relationship is free from idolatry and a person recognizes God as the source of everything. The moment we look to someone to be the source of supplying our happiness or comfort, we put them in the place of God. At that point, loving that person with the love of God becomes an impossibility.

Your theological foundation is crucial to your growth in love. What you believe about God dictates your perspective and attitudes toward people and circumstances in life. If you have misinformation about God, your view of people and situations in life will be skewed.

For instance, if you have been taught that God is good, and your definition of good is *that which makes you happy and comfortable*, then your perception of troublesome people and tragic events will be wrong. Consequently, you'll react negatively.

For many years of my life I struggled in my relationship with God as well as with others because of the man-centered view of God which formed my frame of reference for life. I had accepted a view of a god who had man-like qualities, who had similar thoughts and ways, and had the same value system as most twentieth century, middle-class Americans.

I had a wrong concept of God's goodness: *that which makes me happy and comfortable*. If good things happened, then I felt that God was good. But there are severe problems with such a concept of God's goodness. What is God when tragedies occur? When bad people do bad things, what are we to think about God? We'll discuss this more in later chapters, but for now let's consider your basic beliefs about God.

Basic Beliefs

Your theological foundation, therefore, is crucial to your being equipped to love. How do you answer the following questions? How many gods do you believe exist? Who is God? What does it mean to be God? What is the significance of our being God's creatures in His creation?

In answer to the above, you probably believe there's one God. Most churchgoers are familiar with the Scripture declarations, "Hear, O Israel! The Lord is our God, the Lord is one!" (Deuteronomy 6:4) and, "I am the Lord your God…You shall have no other gods before Me" (Deuteronomy 5:6-7) and, "For I am God, and there is no other" (Isaiah 46:9).

When asked about who God is, you might respond by declaring that Jesus Christ was God in the flesh and is God enthroned. Most believe that Jesus Christ is God and might cite these popular verses: "In the beginning was the Word, and the Word was with God, and the Word was God….And the Word became flesh, and dwelt among us, and we beheld His glory, glory as of the only begotten from the Father, full of grace and truth" (John 1:1, 14), "And Jesus said, 'I and the

Father are one'" (John 10:30), "And He is the radiance of His glory and the exact representation of His nature, and upholds all things by the word of His power. When He had made purification of sins, He sat down at the right hand of the Majesty on high;…" (Hebrews 1:3).

You may assert along with most orthodox Christians that the primary quality or characteristic of being God lies in the fact that all things come from Him and are completely within His jurisdiction and control. We read in I Corinthians 8:4-6, "…we know that there is no such thing as an idol in the world, and that there is no God but one…yet for us there is but one God, the Father, from whom are all things, and we exist for Him; and one Lord, Jesus Christ, by whom are all things, and we exist through Him." And in Colossians 1:16-17, "For by Him [Jesus] all things were created, both in the heavens and on earth, visible and invisible, whether thrones or dominions or rulers or authorities--all things have been created by Him and for Him. And He is before all things, and in Him all things hold together."

God's purpose is to glorify Himself and make Himself known through the revelation of His Son, Jesus Christ. Thus, as His creatures, we are in the humble position of existing completely for His benefit and glory. All creatures wait upon God for their physical and spiritual life. *There are no other sources of supply*. That is clear in the verses above, but also Psalm 104:24, 27-30 affirms our dependence upon God for all things. "O Lord, how many are Thy works!…*They all wait for Thee*, to give them their food in due season. Thou dost give to them, they gather it up; Thou dost open Thy hand, they are satisfied with good. Thou dost hide Thy face, they are dismayed; Thou dost take away their spirit, they expire, and return to their dust. Thou dost send forth Thy Spirit, they are created; and Thou dost renew the face of the ground."

Although the following list is not an exhaustive description of all our beliefs about God, it expresses some that are primary and applicable to our lives on a daily basis.

Basic Beliefs About God

- God is sovereign: He is the first cause of all actions and never reacts to His creation.

- God is holy, good, light, and love.
- God does everything in accordance with His purpose
  ⇒ for His glory.
  ⇒ for His good.
  ⇒ to reveal Christ, His Son.
  ⇒ to make His children more like Jesus: humble and obedient.
- God gives His children everything they need to fulfill His purpose.
- God wastes nothing.
- God's actions are done in perfect wisdom.

Since these are so crucial to our lives we might expect Satan to continually test us at these very basic points. Sometimes a gulf lies between what professing believers say and what their lives reveal about what they really believe. I remember a phrase which circulated around a church I attended which puts it quite bluntly. "You practice what you believe; all the rest is just religious talk." I'm not sure who coined it, but it drives home an important observation.

When it comes to loving, people's actions or responses to others' actions reveal their true doctrinal foundation and motivations. I've noticed that more often than not, when people have a difficult time loving, it is because an idolatrous spirit hinders them. Although they would say they believe in God, they are looking to others to supply something to them in their own way and/or timing. They don't believe that what they receive in other people or circumstances has come to them from the hand of God for a good purpose. Consequently, they begin to try to *use* the other person or *get* the other person to change or supply things in *their* own way and time. Frustration and bitterness ultimately result in such relationships. This confirms that idolatry and love are hostile to each other and are mutually exclusive.

In Psalm 33:13-15 we read these mind-blowing, man-humbling words: "The Lord looks from heaven; he sees all the sons of men; from His dwelling place He looks out on all the inhabitants of the earth, *He who fashions the hearts of them all*, He who understands all their works." It's so tempting to criticize and complain about people as if *they* were the ultimate determiners of *their* condition and *our* happiness. Let's

31

remember: should God decide to remove His restraining hand of grace on us and thereby unleash the evil inside of us which we so quickly abhor in others, we could be worse than they.

These verses assure us that God has fashioned the hearts of everyone to whom we relate. We know that at any given moment He could change them--if it pleased Him and fit His purposes. Although we may not understand all His purposes, we may confidently thank God for the attitudes and actions of those around us because we *believe* God is in control and working all things according to a great and wonderful purpose--to glorify Himself through His Son. If we're believers in Jesus Christ, we know that God is working to glorify His Son in *us*.

In *The Philadelphia Confession of Faith,* which is a book of basic Christian beliefs adopted by the Baptist Association of Philadelphia in 1742, God's ordination of the affairs of His creation is defined.

> God hath decreed in himself, from all eternity, by the most wise and holy counsel of his own will, freely and unchangeably, all things whatsoever come to pass; yet so as thereby is God neither the author of sin, nor hath fellowship with any therein, nor is violence offered to the will of the creature, nor yet is liberty, or second causes taken away, but rather established....[1]

For His people, He works all things (circumstances and relationships) for the purpose of making His people more like His Son, Jesus Christ. In Romans 8:28-29, the apostle Paul wrote, "And we know that God causes all things to work together for good to those who love God, to those who are called according to His purpose. For whom He foreknew, He also predestined to become conformed to the image of His Son, that He might be the first-born among many brethren." Believers in the Lord Jesus Christ have the confidence that their God, the only God, controls all things in their lives, and they have no need to idolize or look to anyone else in life to supply what they need. *Whatever they have at any particular moment is exactly what they need!* It may not be what *they want*, but it is exactly what *they need* to be conformed to the image of Jesus Christ.

Let's get practical for a moment with a hypothetical situation. Johnny's having a hard time understanding his math lesson. Mom tries numerous ways to "get it to him," and each attempt falls short of her goal. How is Mom to love Johnny?

If this mom by the prompting of the Holy Spirit applies the above foundational beliefs about God, she might think this: "Johnny's inability to understand has come to *us* from God and is what *we* need to demonstrate the love of Christ. Johnny's need has made *us* needy for Christ. Thank You, Father, for Johnny's blindness right now. Lord Jesus, fill me with Your patience and love in order that I might glorify You in this situation. What wisdom can You give me that I might discipline or encourage Johnny toward You?"

This same response may be applied to every relationship or circumstance. Whether it's a tired (or energetic) wife, an unreasonable (or understanding) husband, a rebellious (or obedient) teen, or a stingy (or generous) employer; all things come from God in order to lead us to Christlikeness. The moment we begin to look to a person to make us happy or comfortable, at that moment we give him the power to make us miserable. The only way someone can make us miserable, frustrated, or angry is for us to look to him to supply something we want (which is idolatry). Consequently, we can't love him.

Beware of Unbelief

How easily we may fall into the snare of idolatry through unbelief! The writer of Hebrews cited unbelief in God's sovereign administration of all things through Jesus Christ as the sin which so easily entangles us (Hebrews 1:3; 3:12; 8:1; 12:1). It trips us up as we run the course set before us. Only when one fixes his eyes on Jesus does he find the grace to "strengthen the hands that are weak and the knees that are feeble." Have you been entangled in the web of unbelief in God's wise, loving administration of your life--from the tiniest things in your day, to the people with whom you come in contact, to national governments and policies which affect the entire world?

No one knows better than God what situations and people best expose your selfishness, lust, and pride. There have been numerous times when a husband and wife have taken turns informing me of the condition of their relationship. Very seldom do they agree as to who is to blame for the problems. After voicing their complaints, they wait to see with whom I'm going to align. Usually, to their surprise, I suggest that they are perfect for each other and are fulfilling God's purposes in each other's lives. Her selfishness worked perfectly to expose his selfishness and the effects of the spirit of idolatry, and his selfishness worked perfectly in the same way in her life. God knew they were best for each other! Though we are not accustomed to thinking this way, they needed and deserved each other. When two people realize their idolatry, get in touch with their manipulative motives, and crucify the old relationship, God gives birth to a new relationship. As they see God as the wise supplier of all things and give Him thanks, they find a fresh new love flowing between them.

The same is true for the parent-child relationship. What a glorious day it was when Alma and I confessed our idolatry to our children! They could discern that the rod and reproof were nothing more than carving tools employed to make them please us. (The rod should not be used to carve, but to obey God's Word. Parents should discipline their children with the rod, not to get them to obey or to break their stubborn wills, but because God says to do it. We're to trust God to change their hearts. God may supply us with a stubborn child to see if we will obey His Word and trust Him. Will we love the child and obey God's Word, or will we seek our own way?)

As we released them from the demands of our self-significance and pride, we could see the barriers between us disappear before our eyes. Hardness gave way to softness. The distance between us vanished. For the first time, they could tell we accepted them as valuable gifts from God--without performance. How quick most children are to forgive!

I've heard many testimonies from parents who repented of idolatry and accepted their children as perfect gifts from God for leading them to Christlikeness. As God turned the hearts of the parents toward their children in love, so He turned the hearts of the children to their parents just as He promised in Malachi 4:6. "And he will restore the hearts of the fathers to their children, and the hearts of the children to their fathers, lest I come and smite the land with a curse."

Are You Idolizing Anyone?

You can't love someone you idolize. Understanding and applying this principle to relationships brings great freedom to love. I hope you can also see why so many relationships suffer. How are we to remember to consider this? I've found that I need the Holy Spirit's prompting and filling. If we could love without the Spirit of Christ, what proud people we would be, and Jesus would receive no glory. God perfects His love in us as His Spirit examines the motives of our hearts, leads us to distinguish between His kind of love and the world's kind of love, and exposes the deceptive, often hidden spirit of idolatry influencing our words and actions.

Has God revealed the motives of your heart to you as you've read this chapter? God has graciously provided forgiveness for the sin of idolatry through the suffering and death of Jesus Christ. In and through His death, you may receive forgiveness for your sins. Also, in Jesus' resurrection life, you may have fellowship with Him on a daily basis. Furthermore, God promises to give His Holy Spirit to those who ask. If God is revealing Himself to you and you see your need of Him, then God may be calling you to Himself! God may use this book to lead you into a deeper relationship to Him. As truths or ideas strike your conscience and enlighten your soul about your relationship with God, I encourage you to express your heart to Him. Anywhere in this book the Lord Jesus could beckon to you, "Come to Me, all who are weary and heavy-laden, and I will give you rest. Take My yoke upon you, and learn from Me, for I am gentle and humble in heart; and you shall find rest for your souls. For My yoke is easy, and My load is light" (Matthew 11:28-30). When and if He does--*go to Him!* Your relationship with Jesus is foundational to your being equipped to love.

Because Jesus lives, He gives His Spirit to His children in order that His love may be perfected in them. The Holy Spirit knows that all things come from God. He reveals God's purposes behind relationships and circumstances. Jesus, who was/and is the antithesis to idolatry, equips us to love. *He'll remind you: You can't love anyone you idolize.*

Understanding these first two lessons about loving relationships will free you to grow in your love for God. *Continually pray for grace to receive all things and all people as expressions of God's love for you because God purposely brings them to you to provide opportunities for you to reject the spirit of idolatry and turn to Him for the power to love.* When we doubt God's love for us as He ordains the affairs of our lives, we separate ourselves from the grace of God to love and from the ability to respond to life in a God-honoring way. To grumble about circumstances or refuse to give thanks to God for people and their weaknesses, regardless of how inconvenient or hurtful, declares our unbelief in Jesus' lordship and sets us in opposition to His sovereign Word.

If we're to keep our relationships free from a spirit of idolatry, it certainly would be helpful to know more about how to recognize that destructive, deceptive spirit. What are the characteristics of the spirit of idolatry? As the Holy Spirit inspired the writing of the Scriptures, one particular passage offers helpful insight into the devilish characteristics of idolatry--the Ten Commandments.

If we study Deuteronomy 5:6-9 and consider what characteristics are diametrically opposed to what is commanded, we have a description of the spirit of idolatry. In part two, we will examine these verses and learn to recognize the seven characteristics of this spirit in our relationships with God and others.

PART TWO

The Seven Characteristics of Idolatry

Chapter 3

More Than One God

Characteristic #1
The spirit of idolatry proposes that there is more than one god or source of supply for our needs.

Deuteronomy 5:6 *I am the Lord your God*, who brought you out of the land of Egypt, out of the house of slavery. You shall have no other gods before Me.

The Lie

I f there is only one God, one Source of supply of all things, then Satan's chief lie persuades men to look to any source of supply other than God as a dishonor to God and His truth. The father of lies has used the same strategy since the beginning of time. In the garden of Eden there were two trees which represented life and death. The tree of life, representing Jesus Christ, produced fruit which would have given eternal life.

> Then the Lord God said, 'Behold, the man has become like one of Us, knowing good and evil; and now, lest he stretch out his hand, and take also from the tree of life, and eat, and live forever...' (Genesis 3:22).

The second tree, the tree of the knowledge of good and evil, offered a death-producing fruit. God graciously warned Adam, "From any tree of the garden you may eat freely; but from the tree of the knowledge of good and evil you shall not eat, for in the day that you eat from it you shall surely die" (Genesis 2:17). God didn't say He would kill Adam if he ate of it, but that the eating of it would kill him. Why? I believe one reason is because it would alienate him from the tree of life.

Who knows better than Lucifer that looking to something other than God, regardless of how good it is, leads to death? He successfully marketed the earthly product with the same delusion of today's advertising.

> And the serpent said to the woman, "You surely shall not die! For God knows that in the day you eat from it your eyes will be opened, and you will be like God, knowing good and evil" (Genesis 3:4-5).

The spirit of idolatry is a deluding influence. It promotes that which is false. It promises fulfillment and happiness from that which is not God (regardless of how good it appears or how wonderful the experience). We read in 2 Thessalonians that God sends such a deluding influence in order to reveal those who are His and those who are not His.

> And then that lawless one will be revealed whom the Lord will slay with the breath of His mouth and bring to an end by the appearance of His coming; that is, the one whose coming is in accord with the activity of Satan, *with all power and signs and false wonders, and with all the deception of wickedness for those who perish, because they did not receive the love of the truth* so as to be saved. And for this reason God will send upon them a deluding influence so that they might believe what is false, in order that they all may be judged who did not believe the truth, but took pleasure in wickedness (2 Thessalonians 2:8-12).

The spirit of idolatry does not recognize that all things come from one God, but instead suggests that there is more than one source of supply.

Our problem is made worse by our inability to detect selfish motives. Proverbs 16:2 states, "All the ways of a man are clean in his own sight, but the Lord weighs the motives." We humans tend to be concerned about achieving a life of personal happiness, comfort, and affluence. Consequently, we don't know how to pray, or worse yet, we don't care to learn. James, the apostle, wrote that some don't receive because they don't ask, and when they do, they ask with wrong motives (James 4:2-3). Some don't pray much at all, which exposes the underlying belief that God isn't much needed. Others pray quite a bit, but not often that God will be revealed, exalted, and glorified in a situation, or that they will be vessels of His love and mercy. The spirit of idolatry appeals to the selfish motives of the heart.

Our desires to be happy, to look good, and to have wonderful experiences are reinforced by a wrong idea about God and His purposes. An important aspect of Satan's delusion involves false thoughts about God. If it worked on Eve in her unfallen state, imagine how susceptible we are to the idea of a god who has the same vision in life for us as we do--that of making us happy and comfortable. *The inborn spirit of idolatry skews our thinking regarding our purpose in life and God's purposes in creation.* This has caused us to look to things other than to the God revealed in the Bible when we're in need or suffering. Our motives surface when God's purposes call for hardship, suffering, and neediness.

The Truth

With these things in mind, let's contrast how it glorifies God in Jesus Christ for His people to look to Him as their Source of life on a daily basis, event by event, relationship by relationship. He alone has the wisdom to know what we need to become like Christ and for His purposes to be fulfilled in our lives. He sees clearly our sinful motives and therefore can expose them through trials and uncooperative people, which effectively lure our unseen selfishness out of hiding. We may apply what we're told by the Lord Jesus in the Sermon on the Mount, that God knows what we need before we ask Him (Matthew 6:8). But what we need isn't what *we think* we need.

The apostle Paul commented on the believer's response to suffering when he wrote, "And in the same way the Spirit also helps our weakness; for we do not know how to pray as we should…" (Romans 8:26). What is our weakness? Our self-centeredness and inborn idolatrous spirit leads us to ask God to get us out of the suffering or change those who are causing us discomfort or inconvenience. Unless we know God's purpose for us and can recognize the spirit of idolatry, we will not realize that those people or circumstances *are* God's provision for us.

It's a comfort to know that God doesn't condemn us for our weakness, but instead sends us His Helper. Paul continued in Romans 8:26, "…but the Spirit Himself intercedes for us with groanings too deep for words…" Praise God for the ministry of His Spirit! He prays for us when we pray ignorantly or under the influence of the spirit of idolatry. Although we don't know how to pray, the Holy Spirit knows exactly what to pray so that we might become like Christ.

But the Holy Spirit isn't alone in His intercession. Verse 27 continues, "…and He who searches the hearts [Jesus Christ] knows what the mind of the Spirit is, because He intercedes for the saints according to the will of God." Jesus Christ's ministry of intercession also functions effectively even when we pray errantly. When we pray, the Holy Spirit prays, and Jesus understands His requests and enters into intercession before the Father. He always prays according to the will of God, which is that we might be conformed to His image through the situation or relationship which is causing us inconvenience or suffering.

Everything Comes From God

Have you ever considered that everything that happens to you as a child of God comes to you from God? Let's be thorough in our theology and apply it to our lives. *There's only one God from whom all things flow.*

According to Hebrews 7:25, Jesus "always lives to make intercession for us." That's His job twenty-four hours a day, seven days a week, fifty-two weeks out of the year for your lifetime. He never takes a break! We also know that when He prays, all of His prayers are answered one hundred percent of the time because He always "intercedes for the saints according to the will of God" (Romans 8:27). Therefore, we may joyfully and confidently know that whatever occurs in our lives is a direct answer to Jesus' intercession, for Paul continued, "And we know that God causes *all things* to work together for good to those who love God, to those who are called according to His purpose" (Romans 8:28).

What was Paul saying in Romans 8:26-29? In summary, he said that we don't know how to pray, but the Holy Spirit prays when we pray. And Jesus prays according to the intercession of the Holy Spirit and according to God's will. Then God works all things in accordance with their intercession for the purpose of conforming us into the image of His Son. *The spirit of idolatry does not believe that truth and suggests that more than one god exists.*

Just knowing and recognizing this first characteristic of idolatry helps us to see how only Jesus Christ can equip us to love. He never was fooled by Satan's marketing pitches. With confidence and peace He daily walked in the truth that His Father was God and the Source of all things. Whether a miraculous healing or the excruciating pain of the crucifixion, the Lord Jesus Christ maintained His upward look.

The apostle Paul longed for the Colossians to come to the true knowledge of God's mystery, that love and understanding come from Christ, *Himself*, "in whom are hidden all the treasures of wisdom and knowledge" (Colossians 2:2-3). If you're to love, it will flow out of the life of Jesus in you as fruit of the tree of life from Whom you eat. In Jesus' last message to His disciples recorded in the gospel of John, chapters 14-16, Jesus spoke hopeful words to their troubled hearts. In summary, He said,

- ♦ Believe in God.
- ♦ Believe in Me.
- ♦ Abide in Me by eating My word.
- ♦ Abide in Me by praying about all things.
- ♦ Abide in Me by obeying Me--love one another.

♦ I'll not leave you alone to do it; I'll love through the Holy Spirit in you.

In contrast, the spirit of idolatry won't lead you to believe in God or that Jesus Christ is God. It doesn't encourage you to feed on God's Word, pray about all things, or love. But it will catalog *the knowledge* of this first characteristic in your memory banks and lead you to believe that in having the knowledge, you have eaten the best fruit. There's a big difference in having the knowledge about God and living *in Him.* The spirit of idolatry will lead you to believe that in the acquisition of knowledge you are eating of the tree of life. In reality, though, you will have eaten only of the good side of the tree of knowledge.

The tree of life or the tree of knowledge--from which do you eat? How susceptible are you to Satan's marketing scheme? Do you recognize the influence of this spirit in your life? If so, why not bow in the presence of God and confess this characteristic of idolatry?

Believing that there is only one God who is working all things together for good is the basis for a life of thanksgiving. Giving thanks to God for *all* the events and the people in your life expresses your faith in Him and is the equivalent of eating from the tree of life. Also, ask the Lord Jesus to love His Father through you and to convict you when there is evidence of the influence of the spirit of idolatry which looks to anything but God as the Source of life. Remember:

♦ *He alone* **is the Source of supply for all that you need in every situation and relationship.**
♦ **Look to Him as your Source of supply when in need.**
♦ **Realize that what you are supplied by God is exactly what you need to fulfill His purposes and glorify Him.**

Chapter 4

Controls and Carves

Characteristic #2

The spirit of idolatry attempts to manipulate or control people and situations.

Deuteronomy 5:8a You shall not *make* for yourself an idol…

Ted and Cindy were attending their first pre-marriage counseling session. The counselor asked Cindy, "What do you do when you want Ted to do something for you?" Without a moment's hesitation, she replied, "I just smile and look cute." Ted's jaw dropped. A look of "I've been used" came over his face. And he had been!

But Ted wasn't without his means, either. When questioned, he also had some manipulative schemes up his sleeve. That's how idolaters *make* their idols. The counselor sought to lead them to discover the basis for their relationship so they could learn to love. Ted's and Cindy's relationship began under the influence of the spirit of idolatry. Had they continued into marriage without knowledge of the destructive seeds within, their marriage probably would have ended in divorce. They were making idols of one another.

God warned Israel not to "make" idols for themselves. Idols have to be "made" by the idolater because the object of their worship isn't God. *To worship someone is to look to them to supply what only God can supply.* For instance, when Satan tempted Jesus by offering Him the whole world and its glory, Jesus responded, "It is written, 'You shall worship the Lord your God and serve Him only.'" For Jesus to

45

have looked to the devil to supply anything would have been tantamount to worship, and God's Word expressly forbids such sin.

When we look to a creature, an object, or an idea to be the source of provision, comfort, happiness, or power, we are worshiping an idol. *Someone under the influence of the spirit of idolatry seeks to fashion the person or situation to supply self-centered desires and comfort.* Subsequently, it, he, or she becomes the object of manipulation and control. As in the Old Testament days, when an idolater took a knife in hand to make an idol to worship, so we have sophisticated carving tools to make our idols. These "sophisticated" tools aren't new inventions of modern man. They have been around since the Fall in the Garden of Eden. Once you learn to recognize them, you'll see them in many Bible stories.

Mankind has a vast array of carving tools from which to choose. *Carving tools are words or actions designed to get someone to do what we want them to do when we want them to do it.* I've recognized two categories of carving tools: positive and negative.

Positive Carving Tools

When we use something which we know others would like, we're using positive carving tools. Cindy's "smile and look cute" tool worked great on Ted. When she used it, Ted thought Cindy loved him. On the surface of the relationship, everything felt positive, but in reality, Cindy was out to *get* Ted to supply something *she wanted* when she didn't think God was supplying for her.

That's what makes the sin of idolatry so diabolical and deceptive. It makes darkness look like light and deceives the undiscerning person. The spirit of idolatry, when it takes a positive carving tool in hand, also deceives the idolater regarding his own sin. He usually focuses on the other person's fault in not making him happy. Additionally, using a positive carving tool doesn't "feel" like other sins. When the spirit of idolatry influences us in such a "positive" fashion, the guilt rarely registers on the conscience. (Even the victim may not recognize it.)

Although I'm ashamed to admit it, my wife, Alma, and I began our relationship under the influence of the spirit of idolatry. I don't think our story is unusual. Perhaps you can relate as I share our experience.

Alma and I met each other when we were sixteen, juniors in high school. As I looked over the young ladies in our church youth group and high school, I convinced myself (without much effort!) that Alma could really make me happy. From the time I met her, I began carving--positively. If she was in the room, she got my undivided attention. I complimented her hair, her dress, and her abilities. If she ever looked my way, she was always greeted with a smile. As we got to know one another, I began to take her out and do things I knew she would enjoy. I wanted her to think that I really cared for her.

I cared for her, all right. I cared that she be the one to make me happy! I cared to be seen with her. I thought she confirmed my blossoming manhood, since she was a cheerleader and the most beautiful girl I'd ever seen. In my opinion she was one of the top picks in the school and church, and I thought she would be a great helpmeet. Also, her father was the pastor of our church. If I was seen with her, it would perhaps imply that I was spiritually okay. There were many reasons why I thought Alma Hall could meet my needs and make me look good. But all of them were rooted in idolatry. I wanted her for what she could give me, not for how she could draw me into a deeper relationship with Jesus Christ.

Alma didn't know (nor did I) what was motivating all those positive words and actions. She thought I loved her. I was sure I loved her. So as she scanned the church, high school, and college manscape looking for her white knight, I rose to the highest point in her mind. After much carving on my part, she began to think that I was capable of making her happy. My carving was returned with some positive carving of her own. She would wear her hair like I wanted. The clothes I complimented were worn more frequently. She smiled and looked beautiful. I shot rubber bands with notes written on them to her in choir as she played the piano. Then she stretched them out on the piano bench to read them and rewarded me with a look of approval. Sometimes she even shot them back!

After four years of this mutual carving, we were convinced we were right for each other. I was absolutely sure that Alma had the same vision in life as I: making *me* happy! She was convinced I had the same vision in life as she: making *her* happy!

We were in for a rude awakening. I've wondered if God thinks that one idolater deserves another. Within a short time, it became obvious we had fooled ourselves and each other. I was looking to her to supply my happiness and comfort, and she was looking to me for the same. The spirit of idolatry with its positive carving had set the stage for the full-scale destruction of our marriage. We had misinterpreted the positive carving of idolatry as love.

Negative Carving Tools

As our marriage relationship continued, it didn't take long for us each to begin wielding our negative carving tools. *Negative carving tools are words or actions also designed to get others to do what we want, when we want.* Unlike the positive instruments, they are perceived as destructive or hurtful.

The apostle Paul listed six such tools in the third chapter of the book of Colossians. By the way, this chapter stands out as one of the most insightful regarding the sin of idolatry. Assuming that his readers had repented of idolatry (Colossians 3:5-7), Paul encouraged them that they should lay aside their negative carving tools.

> **Colossians 3:1** If then you have been raised up with Christ, keep seeking the things above, where Christ is, seated at the right hand of God. [God is the supplier of all things.]
> **Colossians 3:2** Set your mind on the things above, not on the things that are on earth. [Idols are things on earth. They aren't the source of supply in life. Why?]
> **Colossians 3:3** For you have died and your life is hidden with Christ in God. [Jesus supplies everything you need for life and godliness].
> **Colossians 3:4** When Christ, who is our life, is revealed, then you also will be revealed with Him in glory. [God's purpose for us is not our comfort, but our sharing His glory.]
> **Colossians 3:5** Therefore consider the members of your earthly body as dead to immorality, impurity, passion, evil

desire, and greed, *which amounts to idolatry*.

Colossians 3:6 For it is on account of these things that the wrath of God will come, [Idolatry is a serious sin.]

Colossians 3:7 and in them you also once walked, when you were living in them. [Before we became Christians, the spirit of idolatry ruled our lives.]

Colossians 3:8 But now [now that you have repented of idolatry and looked to God alone as your supplier] you also, put them all aside: anger, wrath, malice, slander, and abusive speech from your mouth.

Colossians 3:9 Do not lie to one another, since you laid aside the old self with its evil practices,...

Six Negative Carving Tools

Anger	**Malice**	**Abusive Speech**
Wrath	**Slander**	**Lying**

Idolatry is the Root

Why do people get angry, display their temper, do mean things to others, destroy others' names, curse and demean with destructive words, and lie? They do these things to *get*! These carving tools are used when the positive ones don't work. They think they can get people to do what they want when they want. In fact, they use the negative ones because they do work--for a while.

Many people struggle against anger in their relationships. They repent of anger time and time again. The reason for the continued bondage lies in their not getting to the heart issue. The root of the problem isn't the anger, it's the idolatry of that individual or situation.

Phil sought counsel regarding his anger. In search of who or what the spirit of idolatry had focused upon, the counselor asked about Phil's childhood. Phil told of his adoption and how his adopted family would meet together and leave him out. As a little boy, he would go to his room during those times and straighten his closet, line up his models on the shelves, and then sit and worship the order he had created.

His idol was "order" because his life was out of order. After years of practicing his idolatry, he married and found himself with four children under the age of eight. You can probably imagine the disorder that came with the little ones. When Phil noticed things out of order in his home or family, he would get angry and storm out to his garage where he worked. There he had created another idol of order. Everything was in its place. *He could control it.*

The root of Phil's anger lay with the idolatry of the idea and feeling of order. His anger was a negative carving tool used to manipulate his wife and children into performing as he wished. When they conformed to his expectations, his anger subsided, but the guilt remained. His primary problem wasn't anger, but idolatry. To experience freedom to love his wife and children, he had to turn from looking to order for peace and comfort. He also had to recognize that his wife and children, along with their attitudes and disorder, were at times just what He needed to display the character and love of Jesus Christ. His wife needed him in those times when the children were out of order. If he was to love her, Phil needed to learn to look to God for His supply to love and serve her as she needed. Why did Phil's anger boil when things got out of control?

Idolatry Involves Control

The issue of idolatry involves control. Man in sin, not trusting God, seeks to control his environment and relationships to ensure his own happiness and comfort. But the very thing he wishes to establish-
-control--he loses. Jesus taught, "For whoever wishes to save his own life shall lose it, but whoever loses his life for My sake, he is the one who will save it" (Luke 9:24). The moment we look to anything other than God to supply our needs, we give that person, object, or circumstance the power to make us miserable. Why? Because there's only one God, and nothing else has the power or the resources to satisfy our needs. If we *have* to have something, it then controls us. The fear of not getting what we want when we want it becomes the empowering factor in the relationship.

At this point in relationships another factor enters in: the carving we perform on people drives them away from us. Often, we drive away the people we most need to love--our immediate family members. Have you noticed how sensitive you are to the manipulative motives of others? You know if your husband or wife is trying to get something from you or when the children turn on the charming and respectful attitudes. You detect the carving tools as if you were equipped with special radar sensors. Recognizing this is helpful in understanding why some relationships have suffered separation and estrangement. Could those being "chiseled" have discerned the spiritual destruction from the spirit of idolatry and retreated in self-protection? What do you do when you feel carved on?

Usually we see the carving tools in others' hands but typically are blind to the ones in our own--unless we learn to recognize this characteristic of the spirit of idolatry in our own lives and repent. My prayer is that from this time on, you'll never be the same. If you've understood this characteristic of the spirit of idolatry, you'll be amazed how quickly the Holy Spirit will direct your attention to your motives. I've noticed that I can be mid-swing with one of my positive carving tools toward Alma or one of the children and the Holy Spirit will question, "Norm, what's that in your hand?" I'm so grateful for His assistance. Without the Holy Spirit, I would have whittled my family to pieces because the idolatrous spirit is so deceitful!

Jesus Never Carves

How has Jesus loved you? Jesus' love doesn't involve manipulation devices aimed at moving you to do something for Him. He uses no positive or negative carving tools to get you to please Him. If you're a Christian, aren't you amazed at how He has changed you without your feeling manipulated and controlled?

If you want freedom to love like Jesus, you must lay down those carving tools. Jesus in you would never resort to such tactics in relationships. When you trust that Christ is in control and what you have is what you need, there's no need to carve, manipulate or control. As you relinquish your rights to have things your way and instead rely on Jesus' power to love through you, you'll grow in your love for God and will be encouraged by His presence.

What Are Your Carving Tools?

With what positive tools have you become adept: flattery, insincere praise, service, or gift-giving?   What negative carving tools do you find in your hands: anger, coolness, withdrawal, harsh words, meanness, or lying? Knowing this second characteristic of the spirit of idolatry has helped me detect its presence. I've used many tools! Recognizing this has been very convicting, confirming my need for Jesus Christ. I hope that by God's grace you'll be able to recognize the carving tools you're accustomed to using and remember:

- ♦ **If you're offended by someone or upset with a situation, it reveals that the spirit of idolatry is at work in your motives.**
- ♦ **You don't need to control and manipulate people and circumstances. It hinders your ability to love and isn't like Jesus.**
- ♦ **You can thank God for all things and worship Him in all things.**

What a glorious freedom there is in Jesus Christ! Let us love one another with the same love with which we have been loved.

Chapter 5

More on Carving

I attended a major evangelistic event in Southern California. The message was centered around the second coming of Christ and the wonderful blessing of being a part of God's forever family. As the speaker came to a close, he appealed to the inborn desire every person naturally has to belong, to not miss out, and to be happy. When he asked if anyone would like to join God's "forever family" and get in on the blessings, he asked them to acknowledge their desire by lifting their hands. Thousands raised their hands. Then he asked them to stand and repeat a prayer of invitation, line for line, asking Jesus Christ to forgive them of their sins and to come live in their hearts. After they finished praying, thousands of people clapped their hands and shouted praises to God. The evangelist then assured each of those who prayed that they were now a part of God's "forever family." They could look forward to God's blessing them now and for eternity.

Within myself, I found mixed emotions. I wanted to rejoice for it was probable that some of those thousands who prayed were genuinely born again by God's Spirit. But at the same time, I wanted to stand and shout, "Wait a minute! It's not that simple. Salvation isn't a matter of one's just praying a prayer to get something from God." I wondered how many of that crowd who prayed approached God in the same spirit they did all other relationships--in a spirit of idolatry to get for self. How many people were carving on God to get Him to supply something?

The idea of carving or manipulating can be applied to one's relationship with God. We've considered its application to relationships on the physical plain, but our relationship to God may also be affected by the spirit of idolatry. It affected me. I discovered that my love for God suffered because I also practiced carving on God. Have you ever carved or attempted to manipulate God? Have you ever related to God like an idol? How does someone carve on God?

Decisionism Without the Holy Spirit at Work

James Adams writes about an error common to the twentieth century Church in an article entitled "Decisional Regeneration."

"Decisional regeneration" attaches a certainty of the new birth to a different act [than the error of baptismal regeneration]. This doctrine sees the new birth as the result of a mechanical process that can be performed by man.[1]

Adams further describes how "decisional regeneration" is promoted through what he calls "soul winning conferences."

In these meetings counselors are instructed that successful counseling must conclude with an individual's absolute assurance of salvation. Counselors are often instructed to assure an individual that his salvation is certain because he has prayed the prescribed prayer, and he has said "yes" to all the right questions. If [the counselee] says "yes" to all the questions, he is asked to pray a prescribed prayer and is then pronounced saved.[2]

For the most part this counseling results in an individual being "regenerated" through a decision. This is essentially the same counseling method used in large evangelistic crusades across the world. There are many variations of this type of counseling, but they all have in common a mechanical element such as the repeating of a prayer or signing of a card upon the performance of which the individual is assured of his salvation.[3]

If the Holy Spirit wasn't at work in the heart of the counselee at the time of the presentation and the counselor were unaware of the character of the spirit of idolatry in the heart of an individual or was unfamiliar with the signs of a God-wrought repentance and faith, idolatry toward God could be the motive for praying that prayer of invitation.

Iain Murray describes a method of counseling youth in his book, *The Forgotten Spurgeon*, which illustrates how one might be led to "carve" on God.

> For example, a booklet, which is much circulated in student evangelism at the present time, lays down "Three simple steps" to becoming a Christian: first, personal acknowledgement of sin, and second, personal belief in Christ's substitutionary work. These two are described as preliminary, but "the third so final that to take it will make me a Christian...I must come to Christ and claim my personal share in what He did for everybody." This all-decisive third step rests with me; Christ "waits patiently until I open the door. Then He will come in..." Once I have done this I may immediately regard myself as a Christian. The advice follows: "Tell somebody today what you have done."[4]

Like James Adams, I think "the methods and theology of those who practice "decisional regeneration" need to be examined--not with a malicious spirit, but with a fervent desire that all of God's people may be one in doctrine and practice for the glory of God." Charles Spurgeon, one of the greatest evangelistic preachers of all time, expressed the balance of love for all who are in Christ, but the need to also examine the doctrine and methods of others in the body of Christ.

> The best way to promote union is to promote truth. It will not do for us to be all united together by yielding to one another's mistakes. We are to love each other in Christ; but we are not to be so united that we are not able to see each other's faults, and especially not able to see our own. No, purge the house of God, and then shall grand and blessed times dawn on us."[5]

Perhaps like me, you have known loved ones and friends who have made so-called decisions for Christ but have since fallen away from God and become disillusioned and disheartened. How do you answer when they testify that they have tried God, but He didn't work for them? How are they to be helped?

We've discussed how the spirit of idolatry uses positive carving tools to get people to do things for them. In the same way I think that unless the Holy Spirit exposes, subdues, and silences the spirit of idolatry, it influences someone to carve on God to get something for himself. As we'll discuss in the next chapter, the motive of the natural heart is to get for self. For instance, if acknowledging some facts and repeating a prayer pleases someone whom a child respects and from whom he or she desires approval, the child certainly sees the benefit of following the counsel given. It isn't difficult to see how a loving, respected pastor could lead an entire group of children to make "decisions" for Christ. But have those decisions produced regeneration, or have they set the children up for disappointment and discouragement? Will they not have to learn they are "unbelievers" before they are truly born again?

Adams related one heartbreaking experience where forty "converts" of such counseling were contacted and only one person was found who appeared to be Christian. We, of course, rejoice in the one who was found, but what about the other thirty-nine? "Some may still believe their eternal destinies were determined by their decision to pray that prayer which is a "fatal confidence" if no repentance and faith be wrought in their hearts. Others may have concluded that they had experienced all that Christianity had to offer. Failing to feel or see any lasting changes in their lives, they may have become convinced that Christianity and its offers of the gospel are a fake and that those who believe such things are either self-deluded fanatics or miserable hypocrites."[6]

It is not within the parameters of this book to fully explain the doctrinal errors involved in "decisional regeneration" or expose the methods which produce such discouraging results. The main point is that the spirit of idolatry doesn't limit its influence to our carving on other people, thus hindering our ability to love them. It also may directly affect our relationship with God. You or others whom you know may have suffered the discouragement of having done all that you know to do to please God, but may have not realized that you were under the influence of the spirit of idolatry rather than the Holy Spirit.

When the Holy Spirit is at work, we don't accept facts because another person has convinced us of their truthfulness or pray in order to get God to do something for us. We believe the facts because God has taught them to us. And we pray in order to relate to Him and yield ourselves to Him. Instead of coming to get from God, we come to give to Him. We give Him our lives for His glory and service with an understanding that He has called us to live and suffer for His name sake. The gospel also tells us that He will give us mercy and grace, not because we have done something to please Him, but because He gives mercy and grace to all who come to Him through His Son, Jesus Christ. I am hopeful that there were some that night in Southern California in whom the Spirit of God was at work bringing them to faith in Christ.

The Spirit of Idolatry May Affect Our Love for God

The purpose of the above is to help us understand how our love for God may be affected by the spirit of idolatry. When a person seeks to use God for his own personal "getting," he will become miserable and bitter when God doesn't deliver what he wants when he wants it. Perhaps you've experienced this yourself or know someone who has. If one doesn't understand the root of the problem, he may find himself looking for more carving tools to use on God--like anger and slander.

If you came to Christ by means of a message or methods similar to the one recounted above, please do not necessarily conclude that you aren't saved. However, you should know that you weren't saved because you prayed a prayer or because you raised your hand or did something to get God to save you. You were saved by what God did through His Son, the Lord Jesus Christ, and that salvation was given you through faith in Him. Where did the faith come from? It came as a result of the work of God's Spirit in your heart as He taught you about your sin, Jesus' righteousness, and His atoning work at the cross. The fruit of God's work in your heart is evidenced by the freedom you have to love God and others.

However, if you prayed the prayer of invitation to Christ, and the Holy Spirit is now revealing your true motives and you've not experienced a freedom to love God and others, then perhaps this explains why you've struggled so much and been disillusioned with God and Christianity. You can be assured that the problem hasn't been God's lack of love for you or some unforgiveable sin. It wasn't God's time to reveal the nature of sin and the root of the problem. Perhaps now is the time!

It's been helpful to me to understand that the spirit of idolatry manipulates, controls, and carves on God to get its own way. I hope it is also helpful to you. It may help you when you are ministering to someone who has "tried Jesus" and has felt unchanged. Knowing about how the spirit of idolatry works also helps us to purify our motives for the spiritual disciplines of grace such as prayer, Bible reading, fasting, fellowship with other believers, giving, and serving. We don't do them to get God to work for us, but instead do them because of our relationship with Him and as an expression of our love for Him. At the same time, we can know that these activities are a means by which God gives us grace for living in a way that glorifies Him.

So, when we think about our love relationship with God, we want to be careful

- ◆ **Not to love God with the world's kind of love--to get selfishly.**
- ◆ **Not to carve on God to get Him to work for us.**
- ◆ **Not lead others to carve on God.**
- ◆ **Give ourselves to Him for His glory.**
- ◆ **Believe God is our source of supply for all things.**
- ◆ **Trust in Jesus' substitutionary death and intercessory life for our salvation.**
- ◆ **Lead others to do the same.**

Selfish

Characteristic #3
The spirit of idolatry makes an idol for self.

Deuteronomy 5:8a You shall not make for *yourself* an idol…

T he third characteristic of the spirit of idolatry focuses on the main purpose for having an idol: selfish ambition or gain. From the time we are infants, we want things *our* way in *our* time. Idolatry rejects God's way and timing of supply.

This characteristic is illustrated in the Israelites' journey to the promised land. The people of Israel grew restless after having been delivered from the hands of the Egyptians. They had been camped around Mount Sinai waiting on Moses to return and give them direction. Camped *too* long! So they called Aaron and said to him, "Come, make us a god who will go before us" (Exodus 32:1). They wanted a god for themselves who would move when they wanted to move and who had no will of his own to which they had to submit.

Self always has an ambition, an expectation, or a viewpoint in every situation or relationship. It asks, "How is this going to affect *me*? Why *me*? What do *I* want or like?" Natural man doesn't ask himself, "I wonder how such and such an action is going to affect others?" unless his motive is to enhance his reputation or affirm his view of himself as a nice person. What would make others happy or comfortable?"

The idolatrous characteristic of selfishness is often demonstrated in marriages today. Bill and Julie represent a vast number of couples whose marriages teeter on the brink of disaster due to selfishness. Each is brilliantly in touch with what displeases him or her about the other, but hasn't a clue regarding his or her own selfishness. If they were to seek counseling, the counselor would get one earful of Julie's problems from Bill and fill up the other one with Julie's version of Bill's problems. Each person may have some legitimate complaints, but their perspectives are self-centered.

Self Demands Idols

Why does an idolater make an idol? What motivates us to carve, manipulate, chisel, or control? It's SELF. There's something we want--a career, order, significance, peace, comfort, happiness, ease, or a million other possibilities. And we want it *when we want it*. You'll find that at the heart of most misery, depression, anger, and frustration is a disenchanted, disillusioned, disappointed *self-love*. When God commanded, "You shall not make for *yourself* an idol," He highlighted why we're inclined to make idols. *Self demands idols*.

The Scriptures have a great deal to say on this subject. The description of worldly wisdom found in James 3:14-16 gives further insight.

But if you have bitter jealousy and selfish ambition in your heart, do not be arrogant and so lie against the truth. This wisdom is not that which comes down from above, but is earthly, natural, demonic. For where jealousy and selfish ambition exist, there is disorder and every evil thing.

Self is Opposed to Goodness

The apostle Paul wrote that we ought to lay aside our old selves. In Ephesians 4:22, he admonished, "that, in reference to your former manner of life, you lay aside the old self, which is being corrupted in accordance with the lusts of deceit." The phrase "lusts of deceit" accurately describes the spirit of idolatry. It deceives us into thinking our desires are worthy of fulfillment. It leads us to believe we deserve to be loved, comforted, respected, obeyed, appreciated, and treated fairly.

In Colossians 3:9 Paul encouraged his readers, "Do not lie to one another, since you laid aside the old self with its evil practices." It's difficult for many to acknowledge that all of self's practices fall short of God's standard for good. One might counter with, "Hold it. People who don't know God do a lot of good things for people. How can good things be evil?"

According to the Scriptures, only those words and actions that flow out of the life of Jesus Christ bring glory to God and can be categorized as "good" by God's standards. You may remember that Jesus defined "good" when he responded to one asking him about what he could do that was good. He said, "Why are you asking Me about what is good? There is only One who is good…" (Matthew 19:17). Although this may not stroke our self-images, we may conclude that when it comes to true goodness, apart from Jesus Christ, we can do nothing. Jesus stated this clearly in his last message to his disciples before being crucified.

> Abide in Me, and I in you. As the branch cannot bear fruit of itself, unless it abides in the vine, so neither can you, unless you abide in Me. I am the vine, you are the branches; he who abides in Me, and I in him, he bears much fruit; for *apart from Me you can do nothing* (John 15:4-5).

The Scriptures do not speak of self in a positive light. Paul taught the Romans that the old self was the cause of slavery to sin. He wrote, "Knowing this, that our old self was crucified with Him, that our body of sin might be done away with, that we should no longer be slaves to sin" (Romans 6:6). Self, slavery, sin, and idolatry are like weeds that choke out the beautiful fruit of love.

Self-Interest Opposes God's Interests

If we wish to sincerely love others, we must be on our guard against self-gratification, self-indulgence, self-centeredness, self-significance, self-comfort, and all the other self-sins which drive us to look to others rather than God. Our natural responses reflect man's interests rather than God's. Such was Peter's problem when the Lord Jesus rebuked him as recorded in Matthew 16:21-25.

From that time Jesus Christ began to show His disciples that He must go to Jerusalem, and suffer many things from the elders and chief priests and scribes, and be killed, and be raised up on the third day. And Peter took Him aside and began to rebuke Him, saying, "God forbid it, Lord! This shall never happen to You."

But He turned and said to Peter, "Get behind Me, Satan! You are a stumbling block to Me; for you are not setting your mind on God's interests, but man's."

Then Jesus said to His disciples, "If anyone wishes to come after Me, let him deny himself, and take up his cross, and follow Me. For whoever wishes to save his life shall lose it; but whoever loses his life for My sake shall find it."

Why did Peter react against Jesus' going to the cross? Jesus pointed to Peter's self-interest. After rebuking Peter, Jesus told His disciples to deny themselves and take up their crosses and follow Him. Peter didn't consider the cross a part of "God's wonderful plan" for his life. Neither does anyone caught in the snare of idolatry. Could it be that the church today is avoiding the *application of the cross* to its gospel because it would offend the masses? Crucifying self and laying aside the old self with its evil practices are not popular topics today.

According to Jesus' response to Peter, it appears that self-interest and Satan are closely linked. If we are to experience freedom to love with God's kind of love, we must search out and destroy selfish ambition and motives behind our words and actions and cry out to God to graciously mortify the deeds of our flesh. Once detected, the selfishness may be rebuked as Peter's was. We may need to boldly command, "Get behind me, Satan! That's idolatry."

Jesus' Love is Selfless

In contrast to the self-interest demonstrated by Peter, let's consider Jesus' self-life. What self-life? His self was dissolved in His Father's will. If we're to love unselfishly, it can only come from His life in us. The Scriptures reveal this glorious quality of life in our Lord. In Matthew 26:39, Jesus almost seems human. "And He went a little beyond them, and fell on His face and prayed, saying, 'My Father, if it is possible, let this cup pass from Me; yet not as I will, but as Thou wilt.'" Perhaps like me, you can relate to the "let this cup pass from me" part. But the "not as I will" shows us the heart of love for His Father and sets Him apart from our selfishness.

Jesus was and is amazing! He was so unselfish with His Father that He never acted on His own initiative nor spoke His own words. He didn't defend Himself when accused or abused, never pushed His own way, and always waited on His Father's timing--even to the point of emptying Himself in death. For whom? Himself? No, for His Father and for His people. Amazing! And now He's emptying Himself in intercession for us. And that's why He's our Savior and our Lord.

How could He do that? One way relates to the issue of self. His "self" was fulfilled and complete in His relationship with His Father. He had no need to be selfish because He trusted His Father to take care of Him. Jesus believed that He always had what His Father wanted Him to have and that whatever came His way was what pleased His Father.

And in Him you have been made complete (Colossians 2:10). Love for others overflows out of vessels filled with contentment. We are channels of His love as we empty ourselves and walk in the fullness of Jesus Christ, Who is our Life. As long as you feel that you are lacking something—that you are empty--you will have your carving tools handy and will be vulnerable to making an idol for *yourself*. The words of a hymn, *Channels Only*, written by Mary Maxwell, testify to this wonderful truth that God's love fills us and flows through us.

> How I praise Thee, Precious Savior, that Thy love laid hold
>   of me;
> Thou hast saved and cleansed and filled me, that I might
>   Thy channel be.
>
> Channels only, Blessed Master, and with all Thy wondrous
>   power
> Flowing through us, Thou can'st use us every day and ev-
>   ery hour.

Jesus, fill now with Thy Spirit, hearts that full surrender
  know;
That the streams of living water, from our inner man may
  flow.

When we surrender our self-will to God's will, we are free to love others. That's why Paul admonished his readers that they have to "put it off." The action verb implies a continuous action--keep putting it off. May the Holy Spirit make you more sensitive to the demand of your self, "Come, make for me an idol so I..." And may you find in Jesus Christ the truth that He is your fullness. It's good to know that this fullness isn't a feeling by which we live, but a fact that we appropriate and in which we walk. If what you have right this moment in every situation comes from God (and it does), then you have everything you can possibly need to glorify Him in that situation. You lack nothing. Remember:

- ◆ **Look to God as your source.**
- ◆ **You have everything you need in Him.**
- ◆ **What you have is what you need.**
- ◆ **The spirit of idolatry will try to get you to focus on yourself.**
- ◆ **But the Holy Spirit will lead you into the fullness of Jesus Christ.**

Chapter 7

Looks to the Creature

Characteristic #4

The spirit of idolatry looks to the creature rather than the Creator to supply happiness which only God can supply.

Deuteronomy 5:8 You shall not make for yourself an idol, or any likeness of *what is in heaven above* or *on the earth beneath* or *in the water under the earth.*

I know many of you perhaps thought that your wife or husband was out of this world when you first met him or her, but by now you've discovered that he or she actually falls into the category of one whose likeness is on the "earth beneath" the heavens. This almost seems unnecessary to say, but people are mere creatures with no power to eternally fulfill others. They can't be gods or sources of supply. You just can't squeeze orange juice out of an apple.

The idolaters during the days of Abraham whittled, chiseled, or fashioned raw, natural material into idols. The Psalmist decried the foolishness of those who take something created and worship it.

Why should the nations say, "Where, now, is their God?"
But our God is in the heavens; He does whatever He pleases.
Their idols are silver and gold, the work of man's hands.
They have mouths, but they cannot speak; they have eyes,
but they cannot see; they have ears, but they cannot hear;
they have noses, but they cannot smell; they have

hands, but they cannot feel; they have feet, but they cannot walk; they cannot make a sound with their throat. Those who make them will become like them, everyone who trusts in them (Psalm 115:2-8).

Our Own Creations

We tend to idolize the "works of man's hands." Remember Phil's idol of order which he created in his bedroom and garage? Other works of "man's hands" may be romance and fantasy, which are ideas created in the mind. Some people look to musical and visual creations for power to cope with life. A young mother confessed that the Lord had convicted her of looking to warm, family relationships as an idol. It wasn't the people themselves, but an idea of how those relationships were supposed to feel and be. Others may look to business, stock portfolios, a retirement account, or the government to supply something which only God can supply. Some people look to food, drink, and drugs which have been added to or refined by man's hands to satisfy their natural cravings. Again, these are all created things which have no power in themselves to supply the fullness our souls long for and that only God can supply.

God's Creatures--Other People

Paul wrote to the Colossians that the wrath of God comes because of idolatry (Colossians 3:5-6). In the Old Testament we read of God's pouring out His wrath on His people because they worshiped creatures rather than Him. We often worship or idolize other people. In the Old Testament, we see obvious idolatry--from the nation of Israel toward Moses, Samson toward Delilah, Saul toward David, and David toward Bathsheba.

Although our idols are seldom made of wood or stone, we still use raw, natural material of flesh and bone. The spirit of idolatry tempts man to look to creatures for happiness. Husbands look to wives, wives to husbands, mothers to children, children to parents, employees to jobs and employers, employers to employees, church members to pastors, pastors to church members, and on and on it goes. Every person you meet becomes potential carving material to the spirit of idolatry. All of these fall into the forbidden category of the "earth beneath."

God's Creature--Yourself

But who is it in your life who probably gets carved on the most? Have you thought of *yourself*? How much do you look to yourself to supply what only God can supply? Have you expected yourself to be beautiful, outstandingly skilled, intelligent beyond your peers, successful, popular, able to please parents, grandparents, and society? To whom did you look to make those grades to please your parents and yourself? To whom did you look to hit that home run, win that race, or score that touchdown? Who was relied upon to pull off that first successful interview?

When it comes to relationship with God, the habit of looking to self to perform or choose what God requires doesn't change. Have you looked to yourself to be righteous in God's sight--to perform adequately so as to hush a condemning conscience? Do you expect God to give you eternal life because you made the right choice with your own free will? Or do you think that you deserve God's blessing because you were able to distinguish between good and evil and choose the good?

You and I (if born anew by God's Spirit) are merely creatures-- raw, natural material--sophisticated, divine designs of molecules; but different from all other creatures, given the capacity to know and worship God. From the time we were children, we have chiseled and carved on ourselves to supply according to the expectations of others, God, and ourselves. It only makes sense that we would do so. From the beginning of our lives our parents expected us to be good children. They expected us to behave and control ourselves without the grace of God or relationship with Jesus Christ. So, it should be no wonder that we continue to walk in the way we were trained --looking to ourselves to be like God. I might add here, that it is right for parents to teach their children that they are responsible creatures before God. It is that feeling of responsibility that leads us to see that we can't supply our own righteousness and are in need of a savior. But the Bible clearly teaches that our natural hearts are dead to God, and in the flesh we cannot obey God or please Him.

For the mind set on the flesh is death, but the mind set on the Spirit is life and peace, because the mind set on the flesh is hostile toward God; for it does not subject itself to the law of God, for it is not even able to do so; and those who are in the flesh cannot please God (Romans 8:6-8).

Consider the idea of expecting or desiring to be like God. It was the temptation the serpent dangled before Eve with regards to the tree of the knowledge of good and evil. Eating from that tree represented the power of free choice between good and evil. God declared that in the day Adam and Eve ate of it, they would surely die. Why? Because man looking to himself to determine good and evil alienates himself from the life and power of God--a despising of the Tree of Life in Christ. It's idolatry of self!

Ever since that fateful day in the garden, mankind has tried to usurp God's place and steal His glory. That was the Tempter's purpose in luring Eve to eat of the tree of the knowledge of good and evil and to reject the Tree of Life. It seemed right to Adam and Eve to "be like God" because the prevailing motive of their hearts was to be like God. Knowing and choosing between good and evil surely appealed to our first parents (even as it appeals to us today), but there was one major problem with that--it left out God! Every man (and woman) has made the same fatal choice throughout all history--ignore the Tree of Life in Jesus Christ and put confidence in the creature and his ability to secure life and happiness. We've all eaten from the tree of knowledge and missed the mark of God's righteousness, thereby falling short of God's glory.

I want to be clear about the deception of the spirit of idolatry. It leads us to look to ungodly sources for things which only God can supply. The deception lies in the fact that the source to which we look appears to be able to supply our needs--it looks good! The tree of the knowledge of good and evil stands before each one of us every moment. It seems good and right that we know the difference between good and evil and make the choice for what is good. And it is --*if the revelation and the choice flow out of a relationship with Jesus Christ*.

But we can still choose "good things" for the wrong motives. All of man's choices for good, even choosing to accept the historical facts and testimonies *regarding Jesus Christ*, may be idolatrous if they are made as a matter of pure academics *without a relationship with Jesus Christ*. The idolatry lies in trusting one's natural intellect--thinking that knowing facts is sufficient to merit salvation. Jesus taught his disciples that His Father's teaching and working brings the true believer to faith in Christ. A couple of examples are recorded in John 6 and John 15. The first illustrates how a group came to Jesus, but came without being "taught by God", the Father. The second exemplifies that nothing is done in our lives apart from the Lord Jesus Christ, Himself. The spirit of idolatry would lead us to believe we can do something apart from God's working through His Spirit.

> The Jews therefore were grumbling about Him, because He said, "I am the bread that came down out of heaven." And they were saying, "Is not this Jesus, the son of Joseph, whose father and mother we know? How does He now say, 'I have come down out of heaven'?" Jesus answered and said to them, "Do not grumble among yourselves. No one can come to Me, unless the Father who sent Me draws him; and I will raise him up on the last day. It is written in the prophets, 'And they shall all be taught of God.' Everyone who has heard and learned from the Father, comes to Me." (John 6:41-45).

> I am the vine, you are the branches; he who abides in Me, and I in him, he bears much fruit; *for apart from Me you can do nothing* (John 15:5).

Our ability to love doesn't come from the power of the creature's will any more than our new birth does. Although our wills are active, love comes from God, Himself, as we are taught by Him, relate to Him, eat from Him, abide in Him, and trust in Him. Then He moves us by His Spirit from our hearts, and we choose to love. We do not believe or love God with a faith or love independent of the life of Christ. Paul wrote to the Galatians that "we live by the faith of Jesus Christ" (Galatians 2:20). With the apostle John, we testify that "love comes from God" (I John 4:7). As we humbly acknowledge our sin of idolatry and pursue fellowship with Jesus Christ, we become channels of God's love. To God be all the glory!

We must be careful not to think that God's commandment against looking to creatures or created things for happiness or power implies that we have the ability to choose to obey that commandment without God. Instead, we must realize that we need a constant reminder to cry out to God. That's where the weaknesses, frailties, and sins of others (and ourselves) can be turned into a blessing. They remind us of our own neediness before God. When we recall that our only usefulness to God is as objects and vessels of His love, we find a basis for happiness and the power to love.

It also helps to remember that the value of others is not what they give to us, but that their sinfulness and weakness gives opportunity for Jesus' love to be drawn out of us. We need to look at others as the Creator's provision for us to love and walk according to His Word. Then we will love God more and respond with grateful hearts. When one of His creatures challenges our ability to love and serve unselfishly, we are drawn to Christ either through our failure or through our need. The wonderful invitation from Hebrews 4:16 is appropriately applied in such cases. "Let us therefore draw near with confidence to the throne of grace, that we may receive mercy and may find grace to help in time of need."

The next time you find yourself upset with someone because they didn't do what you wanted when you wanted them to, cry out to God for filling and direction in how to love. Perhaps He'll bring to mind this fourth characteristic of idolatry:

- ◆ **The spirit of idolatry looks to creatures or created things.**
- ◆ **This one can't be my god; he's just a creature given to me for the purpose of drawing me to Christ.**

Chapter 8

Serves Many Idols

Characteristic # 5
The spirit of idolatry serves many idols.

Deuteronomy 5:9 You shall not worship them or *serve them*;

T he apostle Paul wrote to the Romans, "There is none righteous, not even one; there is none who understands, there is none who seeks for God" (Romans 3:10-11). No idolater limits himself to one god. We know there are no other gods but One. But the natural man's idea of God is a misunderstanding of the true God. God gave us insight into the insatiable appetite of the spirit of idolatry when He used the plural in verse 9. Since whatever a natural man looks to isn't God, it won't be long before he'll become dissatisfied and will begin his search for another to supply what he wishes.

By its nature, the spirit of idolatry has lusts unfulfilled. When one's carving doesn't work on the creature of choice, the idolater selects a more pliable or moldable material. He throws one idol off the pedestal of worship, only to replace it with another. Consequently, many people have what I call an "idol trail" of relationships and things strewn behind them from their past.

A Trail of Idols

I think most of us have the same general idol trail. As babies, we looked to Mom to supply what we wanted when we wanted it. How could we know when Mom fed us that it was God supplying through her in His way, His time? Unknowing idolaters that we were, we carved with crying, smiling, throwing tantrums, cooing, and a various assortment of positive and negative implements. The tools which worked were encouraged, and the ones which failed were replaced. But it didn't take long for each of us to realize that Mom wasn't going to have the same interests as we. She came in her way and in her time. So we were compelled to become our own god: responsible for getting what we wanted when we wanted it. In Psalm 115:3 we read, "But our God is in the heavens; He does whatever He pleases." Under the spirit of idolatry man believes *he* is god, and he does whatever he pleases, which is a rejection of the one, true God.

Looking to ourselves as the one to supply happiness in life, we fashioned our idols to serve ourselves. When parents failed us, we turned to our peers. During the elementary and teen years, we perhaps carved on entire classrooms of friends, trying to get them to supply the significance and happiness we felt we deserved. But that's too many people to control all at once, and we probably narrowed the field to a few friends. Friendships developed based upon whether or not they responded positively to our carving and chiseling. If someone was useful to us and gave us what we wanted, then they became our friends; but when they were disloyal, weak, or failed to gratify our desires and ambitions, off the pedestal they went.

By high school, we may have scaled down the field even further to a few select individuals and may have become more creative in our imaginative and fantasy-inspired idols. For girls, the boys who showed evidence of having the same vision in life as they (making them happy), were crowded onto the pedestal of the heart. Maybe they were measured by the idol of romance promoted by movies, songs, TV, and romantic novels. For boys, girls who could be used to make them feel significant or comfortable got the nod. Often these girls were measured by the idols of pornography which had captured a spot on the pedestal during the teen years. As the process of elimination continued, one by one idols were raised and knocked off until one was worthy of worshiping in marriage.

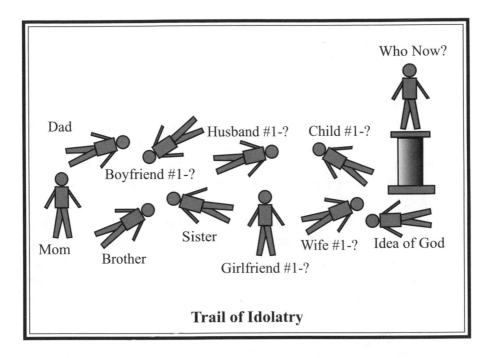

Trail of Idolatry

Marriage only proved that the mate wasn't God and couldn't match up to the idols of romance and pornography. But that didn't stop the spirit of idolatry. Divorce and remarriage may have followed. The sad thing is that the church has somewhat sanctioned such destruction as ministers perform remarriages, not realizing that the root problem for the first divorce was that the two people didn't know how to love. Perhaps there was nothing wrong with the match, but the problem was with the basis for the initial relationship. *Idolatry may be the leading cause of marriage, divorce, and remarriage in the world.*

If God doesn't use this devastation in one's life to draw him or her to Christ and expose the idolatry, the spirit of idolatry continues to set up idols. Wives usually turn their idolatrous tools toward those lovable, assumed-easy-to-mold, little children. Perhaps they think these little ones can provide happiness and opportunities for vicarious satisfaction. But if a mom gets too frustrated with the children, she may seek a career instead.

Husbands typically turn to their jobs. A skilled man can carve on his employer and job through excellent service and performance and get considerable self-gratification in many areas. The issue here is motive. We *are* called upon to perform our jobs well and to be excellent workers. But *why* are we motivated to do excellent work? To honor God? To gain a good reputation for ourselves? To build our own self-image? It is our motives that determine whether our "good work" is actually good from God's perspective.

Men who have idolized pornography may continue to search for more. With pornography, a man can indulge himself without the risk of rejection (except from his wife if she is aware of his idolatry). But what a whirlwind of destruction lies in the wake of an idolatry of pornography.

The idol trail lying in our past cries out for justice. The guilt of selfish living doesn't disappear when the next idol temporarily provides. One might not feel the guilt for a while, but eventually, it takes its toll. Others notice the trail of broken relationships in one's past and the idolater finds himself isolated and unattractive. The law of the harvest--we reap what we sow--starts to kick in.

Somewhere in the midst of all these idolatrous relationships, some may even try to use God. A false idea of God then becomes another discarded idol in the pile of has-beens. Sometimes the pile gets so large that one has to sweep them into a mental closet and shut the door with hopes of avoiding the guilt. But the smell of death permeates the person's life, and he or she is trapped in the mire of miserable relationships. How does this happen? It happens because instead of worshiping and serving God, one...

Worships and Serves Idols

How does one "worship" an idol? Jesus' response to Satan's temptation in the wilderness gives insight into Jesus' understanding of what constitutes worship.

> And he [the devil] led Him [Jesus] up and showed Him all the kingdoms of the world in a moment of time. And the devil said to Him, "I will give You all this domain and its glory; for it has been handed over to me, and I give it to whomever I wish. Therefore if You worship before me, it shall all be Yours."

> And Jesus answered and said to him, "It is written, 'You shall worship the Lord your God and serve Him only'" (Luke 4:5-8).

Jesus understood that His looking to His Father to supply His needs was the essence of worship and service to His Father. Jesus' recital of the command indicates that when He looked to God as His supply and trusted in God's timing for the supply, He was worshiping and serving God.

In the same way, when we idolize someone--look to them to supply what only God can supply--we put that person in the position of being worshiped or served. For instance, when a young man wants to get something from a young woman, he unconsciously finds himself seeking to please her. Her wish becomes his command! In fact, as long as he wants to use her for his own selfish ends, he gives her the power to make him miserable and angry. She actually becomes the lord of his life, and he becomes her servant. He wouldn't dare ignore her desires for fear that he might not get what he wants. These dynamics go on between any idol and its worshiper. The idolater becomes the slave of the idol.

Often this kind of idolatry occurs in marriages. Jeff and Jan went for counseling when their relationship had deteriorated to the point that both were miserable. As they each shared how discontented they were and how empty the relationship had become, they didn't realize that they were testifying to the fruit of an idolatrous relationship. In looking to each other as suppliers of happiness and comfort, they had given to one another the power to make each other miserable. The root of their problem was that they had worshiped each other!

If we look for someone to make us happy, we put them in the powerful position of controlling us. Their pleasures and desires become the object of our efforts in order to get our own pleasures and desires fulfilled. We serve them and seek to please them, expecting that to "work" to our benefit. If our serving them (a positive carving tool) does work, then we're happy campers. This usually occurs in the dating season or beginning of a relationship. But when our idol quits responding to our service, or takes advantage of it and begins to expect to be worshiped and served, look out! We're offended and miserable, hate them for using us, and pull out the negative carving tools. We despise them because we feel they don't love us. If they love us, we rationalize that they should want to serve us. Being deceived by the spirit of idolatry, we feel totally justified in all our actions and thoughts. But we're miserable, and *we have given them the power to make us miserable by idolizing them.*

Subconsciously, we despise ourselves for giving them that control. By the time we've used many idols and felt the misery and guilt of our life-style of worshiping and serving them, we may blame ourselves for lousy choices--but not for idolatry. Instead of dealing with the root problem, we find ourselves becoming more protective of self and less trusting of others. We might even say after a broken relationship or marriage, "I'm never gonna let that happen to me again."

But it does! And it will happen again and again unless there is repentance for worshiping and serving someone other than God alone. There's only one hope for peace and fulfillment: taking responsibility for living to please our biggest idol--ourselves--and for the destruction and hurt caused by idolizing all those people. A glorious freedom and peace comes when we confess our idolatry to God and to those we've idolized. I'm not suggesting that we search out all those old flames of the past, but deal with the habit pattern before God, using specific names and things. Then deal personally with those relationships that are current. Most particularly, I'm thinking of repenting before our parents, spouses (and/or ex-spouses), or children. Praise God for the power of the blood of Jesus Christ which cleanses us from all sin. Through His atoning sacrifice we find peace with God and a basis for healed relationships.

Alma and I experienced great renewal and revival in our marriage as we confessed the sin of idolatry in our previous relationships, as well as in our own. We found our consciences didn't have to strive long and hard to know where to repent. God broke our hearts over the destruction we had caused in others' lives, including our own, because we didn't know how to love. The freedom which came as we confessed idolatrous childhood, junior high, high school, and college relationships was glorious.

God's mercy through the cross of Christ washed our consciences and produced a new vision for our marriage and relationships with our children. We also experienced God's forgiveness in a personal way as we released each other. When we released our children from our idolatrous expectations both in prayer and in open confession to them, a new love entered into our family which healed wounds and bitterness caused by our sin. That process continues on a daily basis.

Jesus Christ left nothing in the wake of His life but healed and transformed people . There were no idols bearing the scars of His manipulations. Also, Jesus was clearly not controlled by anyone but His Father. There was no fear of man, only fear of God. Jesus' perspective was that every person He encountered was from His Father for Him to love. Read what Jesus said of Himself.

> Jesus therefore said, "When you lift up the Son of Man, then you will know that I am He, and *I do nothing on My own initiative*, but I speak these things as the Father taught Me. And He who sent Me is with Me; He has not left Me alone, for *I always do the things that are pleasing to Him*" (John 8:28-29).

The apostle Paul also apparently had a firm grasp on living to please God rather than men. Paul's boldness testified to the fact that no man controlled him because of idolatry. One can't serve Jesus Christ and serve idols simultaneously.

> For am I now seeking the favor of men, or of God? Or am I striving to please men? If I were still trying to please men, I would not be a bond-servant of Christ (Galatians 1:10).

Can you imagine the relief which comes to someone when he or she realizes why his or her life has been filled with miserable relationships? Try! It results in a spiritual high. There's nothing greater than returning to God the worship and service which He deserves. The writer of Psalm 130 says it for all of us who know God.

> If Thou, Lord, shouldst mark iniquities, O Lord, who could stand? *But there is forgiveness with Thee, That Thou mayest be feared*. I wait for the Lord, my soul does wait, and in

His word do I hope. My soul waits for the Lord more than the watchmen for the morning; indeed, more than the watchmen for the morning. O Israel [God's people], hope in the Lord; for with the Lord there is lovingkindness, and with Him is abundant redemption. And He will redeem Israel [His people] from all his iniquities (Psalm 130:3-8).

God is looking for such worshipers--worshipers who fear Him more than men. His people are to treat Him as holy and look only to Him. The apostle Paul apparently called the Thessalonians to turn from their idolatry because He wrote,

For the word of the Lord has sounded forth from you, not only in Macedonia and Achaia, but also in every place your faith toward God has gone forth, so that we have no need to say anything. For they themselves report about us what kind of a reception we had with you, and how you *turned to God from idols to serve a living and true God*, and to wait for His Son from heaven, whom He raised from the dead, that is Jesus, who delivers us from the wrath to come (1 Thessalonians 1:8-10).

Have you ever taken responsibility for the destructive trail of idolatry in your past? I encourage you to turn around and look at the wounded and discarded idols. I realize this may be frightening because it requires letting God shine His light into the "deceitful, desperate wickedness" of our hearts. But the only alternative is to continue living with a nagging feeling of separation from God because of the guilt of idolatry and the powerlessness to love.

The spirit of idolatry serves many idols, but the spirit of love looks only to God. I invite you to take time to pray and write down the names of those to whom you've looked through the years. Then one by one, ask God to forgive you, and to heal each person you've hurt. Then release them from the responsibility of being god to you. May God's power restore and heal broken relationships as you turn from idols to serve the living and true God. Let's remember:

- ◆ We worship and serve someone or something when we look to it to provide what we need when we want it.
- ◆ When we worship and serve someone or something, we give it the power to make us miserable.
- ◆ To turn from idols to worship and serve a living God, we need to take responsibility for the idol trail we've created.
- ◆ If we're going to love as Jesus loved, we must worship and serve only God.

Chapter 9

Reproduces Itself

Characteristic #6
The spirit of idolatry reproduces itself.

Deuteronomy 5:9 You shall not worship them or serve them, for I, the Lord your God, am a jealous God, *visiting the iniquity of the fathers on the children, and on the third and the fourth generations* of those who hate Me,

Reproduces in One's Own Life

S omewhere back in the deep recesses of my mind I recall from my childhood a scene from an old movie or comic book story that involved this "blob-like" creature. Although I don't remember much of the story, the thing that sticks in my memory is that this "blob" continued to grow and destroy everything in its path. That blob reminds me of the spirit of idolatry. It grows and reproduces itself until it destroys everything in one's life.

We can be grateful that God is jealous and judges the idolatry of His people. Usually when we think of God's judgment, we think of punishment. But there is another side to God's judgment where He passes judgment on the sin He sees in our lives. Then, in order to show that His judgment is true, He gives us over to the sin that He sees but we don't see. Apparently, God knows that where idolatry exists unchecked or unrepented of in the souls of men, it reproduces itself and creates more destruction. And the spirit of idolatry takes advantage of every opportunity to express itself. In Romans 1:22-32, we see such dynamics at work.

> Professing to be wise, they became fools, and exchanged the glory of the incorruptible God for an image in the form of corruptible man and of birds and four-footed animals and crawling creatures.
>
> Therefore [because of idolatry] God gave them over in the lusts of their hearts to impurity, that their bodies might be dishonored among them. For they exchanged the truth of God for a lie, and worshiped and served the creature rather than the Creator, who is blessed forever. Amen.
>
> For this reason [because of idolatry] God gave them over to degrading passions; for their women exchanged the natural function for that which is unnatural, and in the same way also the men abandoned the natural function of the woman and burned in their desire toward one another, men with men committing indecent acts and receiving in their own persons the due penalty of their error [homosexuality may result from idolatry].
>
> And just as they did not see fit to acknowledge God any longer [idolatry], God gave them over to a depraved mind, to do those things which are not proper, being filled with all unrighteousness, wickedness, greed, evil; full of envy, murder, strife, deceit, malice; they are gossips, slanderers, haters of God, insolent, arrogant, boastful, inventors of evil, disobedient to parents, without understanding, untrustworthy, unloving, unmerciful; and, although they know the ordinance of God, that those who practice such things are worthy of death, they not only do the same, but also give hearty approval to those who practice them (Romans 1:22-32).

These are just a few of the sins that flow out of "the blob" of idolatry. In Colossians, Paul equated impurity, passion, evil desire, and greed with idolatry (Colossians 3:5). When we give it an inch, it takes a mile.

As the law of the harvest dictates, when idolatry is *sown*, the idolater *reaps* idolatry plus much more wickedness. He reaps it *later* than when he sowed it, and *in greater quantity*. "Do not be deceived, God is not mocked; for whatever a man sows, this he will also reap. For the one who sows to his own flesh shall from the flesh reap corruption, but the one who sows to the Spirit shall from the Spirit reap eternal life" (Galatians 6:7-8).

Beware of the blob! Not only does it reproduce evil in one's own life, but it…

Reproduces in the Next Generation

God said that He visits the iniquity of the fathers on the children, down to the third and fourth generations (Deuteronomy 5:9). Consider the destruction which comes to families from idolatry and the inability to love. Children learn from parents' examples. Those who don't love with God's kind of love provide models of idolatry that the children imitate and practice. As parents idolize themselves, each other, the children, the pastor, their jobs, and a thousand other things or people, the children have no spiritual discernment to recognize it for what it is. Consequently, the children copy the behavior of their parents, and the spirit of idolatry in them begins to feed off of everything around them--just like the blob in the movie.

Furthermore, lifelong practices are passed on to the next generation as parents give hearty approval to their children for the same idolatrous behavior. They encourage it because they don't recognize it as sin. How can they condemn in their children what they don't condemn in their own lives? They teach their children how to be nice to others if they want to be treated nicely. Children learn from their parents how to use both positive and negative carving tools much like they learn how to use a household appliance. They watch how it's done and then try it themselves.

How about in your family? Do you see signs of the spirit of idolatry in your children? Do they carve on you and on their brothers and sisters? Do you carve on them? If you have older children, have you seen the destruction in their marriages and in their families because they don't know how to love? If so, you are witnessing the reality of the sixth characteristic of the spirit of idolatry.

If we're to learn to love, we need to know that God is jealous. He commands us to look to Him for all things and to thank Him for all things. He constantly exposes our inability and unwillingness to look to Him as He ordains difficulties in relationships and circumstances. Everything comes from Him for our conformity to Jesus Christ.

When we look elsewhere, God doesn't shrug His shoulders and turn a blind eye. His jealousy is stirred, and His wrath pours out. In Romans 1:18, we find that God has a settled opposition to sin. His wrath is revealed against *all ungodliness and unrighteousness*. Should He turn His head, mankind would have no basis for confidence that justice reigns in heaven and will eventually also reign on earth. We also wouldn't see our need for a righteousness beyond ourselves.

If we're His children, then God disciplines us that we might learn to love. He withholds the grace to love in order to show us that we need to repent of idolatry. The writer of Hebrews put it this way in chapter 12:5-17:

> My son, do not regard lightly the discipline of the Lord,
> nor faint when you are reproved by Him; for those whom
> the Lord loves He disciplines, and He scourges every son
> whom He receives (Hebrews 12:5-6).

The idea of discipline here is not that of punishment as much as it is of training. As all children do, we need to be trained to trust in God and believe that He is running all things by the "word of His power" (Hebrews 1:3). Idolatry can only take place in an atmosphere of unbelief in God. When we are tripped up by unbelief (the sin "which so easily entangles us" mentioned in Hebrews 12:1), we need to be trained or instructed. We need to see where we got off the course that was set before us and when we fixed our eyes on someone other than Jesus Christ.

> It is for discipline that you endure; God deals with you as
> with sons; for what son is there whom his father does not
> discipline? But if you are without discipline, of which all
> have become partakers, then you are illegitimate children

and not sons. Furthermore, we had earthly fathers to discipline us, and we respected them; shall we not much rather
be subject to the Father of spirits, and live? For they disci-
plined us for a short time as seemed best to them, but He
disciplines us for our good, that we may share His holiness.
All discipline for the moment seems not to be joyful, but
sorrowful; yet to those who have been trained by it, after-
wards it yields the peaceful fruit of righteousness (Hebrews
12:7-11).

How true! When God sends someone into our lives who has the
mission and capacity to draw that spirit of idolatry out in the open, it is
not a joyful time. Rather than finding a place to repent of idolatry and
unbelief in God, our tendency is to avoid the hurtful relationship, seek
to carve the idol into shape, or develop bitterness toward it for messing
up our lives --anything but endure until God's training is completed.
We need the encouragement of these verses, don't we?

What glorious results come from God's Fatherly training--the
peaceful fruit of righteousness! It's peaceful because you are contented
and have learned not to live life to *get*. When you believe in God and
believe that He always gives you what you need to look to Jesus Christ
and be conformed into His image, you enjoy a supernatural and lasting
peace. It's a peace which the world cannot give and that cannot be
stolen. Are you facing this kind of training?

Therefore, strengthen the hands that are weak and the knees
that are feeble, and make straight paths for your feet, so
that the limb which is lame may not be put out of joint, but
rather be healed (Hebrews 12:12-13).

The writer makes an obvious allusion to Jacob, the conniving,
heal-grabbing limper, who wrestled with God. We think our problem
is the person who seems to be bent on making our lives miserable, or
that situation which refuses to be resolved into comfort and happiness.
But the problem is our refusal to worship and serve God only. We
often fail to realize that God has an unwavering goal to sanctify us and
purify us from our unbelief and idolatry. If we're to glorify God in our

lives, we've got to stop struggling, surrender to Christ, and yield to what He's doing in our lives. Instead of wrestling with God (which is sure to leave some visible wound), we need to yield to His purposes.

> Pursue peace with all men, and the sanctification without which no one will see the Lord. See to it that no one comes short of the grace of God [which is, the power to trust and love, especially in the face of offenses]; that no root of bitterness springing up causes trouble, and by it many be defiled; that there be no immoral or godless person like Esau, who sold his own birthright for a single meal. For you know that even afterwards, when he desired to inherit the blessing, he was rejected, for he found no place for repentance, though he sought for it with tears (Hebrews 12:14-17).

The main point of the book of Hebrews is that we are to believe that there is only one God and that Jesus Christ is the radiance of His glory. We're told that Jesus Christ has been raised up and seated at the right hand of the throne of God, where He is running everything by the Word of His power. When we don't believe that Jesus Christ is God and that He is the source of all things, we will look to others to supply what only God can supply. In our idolatry, we don't believe God's Word to us regarding Jesus Christ.

Consequently, this reveals that the bitterness and immorality mentioned in Hebrews 12 stem from idolatry. It is because of idolatry, resulting from our unbelief in God, that we fall short of the grace of God to be holy and be at peace in our relationships or in difficult situations. What is your view of God's control over relationships, personal failures, tragic accidents, sickness, and death?

The Spirit of Idolatry Feeds Upon a Distorted View of God

> For from Him and through Him and to Him are all things.
> To Him be the glory forever. Amen (Romans 11:36).

Yet for us there is but one God, the Father, from whom are all things, and we exist for Him; and one Lord, Jesus Christ, by whom are all things, and we exist through Him. However not all men have this knowledge... (I Corinthians 8:6-7).

Do you believe that all things come from God to carry out His plan to conform us into the image of Jesus Christ? My observation has been that many today who say they believe the Bible actually do not believe this. Many people in the church today have a distorted view of God because the truth about His sovereignty and His purpose for man has been suppressed or reinterpreted to make God believable and acceptable to the hearts of a modern, ego-centered man. The most prominent idea associated with this distortion is that God is not responsible for any of the tragedies or hardships that befall me or other "good Christians" (yet we know if God is God, He could prevent them). Believing in this distortion inevitably causes us to become bitter towards God when things don't go well for us, resulting in more idolatry.

For instance, let's imagine a young man and his girlfriend driving through a valley on a winding, country road. The bright, sunny day, the sweet smell of honeysuckle, trees fully clothed in luscious green, her beautiful face, and interesting conversation have captured the attention of all his senses. Fully engrossed in conversation and the moment, they unknowingly approach the railroad tracks that lie around the next bend in the road. Fifty yards before the tracks, a deer suddenly darts out from the thick brush, and the young man slams on the brakes, narrowly missing the deer and stopping mere feet from the tracks. Simultaneously, a fast freight train barrels through the unguarded crossing. The young couple stare at the roaring train in astonishment. Had he not braked for the deer that the train spooked, they would have collided with the train for sure!

Three different interpretations of this incident reveal one's concept of God. They might be expressed as follows:

1. An unbeliever might say, "Boy, was I lucky!"
2. The modern, man-centered church member might say, "Wow! Praise

God. Satan was trying to kill me with that train, so You had the train spook the deer to save me from the devil's scheme. I know You would never want anything bad to happen to us because You love us. That's why You rescued us from death."

3. The one who is closest to knowing the real God of the Bible might say, "Praise God! Thank You, Lord; You Who are sovereign over me, my girlfriend, my car, the train, and the deer; You Who control and ordain all events to reveal Yourself and to draw Your people into fellowship with You. Thank You for reminding me that You own my next heartbeat and each one after that. Glorify Yourself in this event, Lord, and thankYou for Your great mercy."

If you agree with the second viewpoint, you are eventually going to deal with bitterness toward God. What are you to think when tragedy strikes and the ending isn't so happy? That Satan won? You won't understand that God controls all things in order to glorify Jesus Christ and perfect His faith in His people. You will feel anger toward God whenever God doesn't keep you and your loved ones safe and comfortable. Perhaps you'll be confused at why you, a child of God, apparently have been defeated by Satan. Have you felt this way? This all arises from a misunderstanding of God's sovereignty over events (and all things) and His purpose for creating you.

The spirit of idolatry distorts our view of God and thus reproduces itself in our own lives. As parents or ministers, we then teach that distorted view of God to our children and disciples who, under the influence of the spirit of idolatry, are quick to believe the error.

An Unwanted "Visitor"

When you find yourself unable to love, you are probably experiencing the "visitation" of the iniquity of idolatry. The idea of "visit" in Deuteronomy 5 is that of judgment. God has seen the idolatry in the heart and judges it. He judges it by giving us over to its power so that we might see how we need to repent. This is not the kind of "visitor" we want in our souls!

When you find yourself angry at someone, compelled to point out their transgressions against you so they can repent, and you are

88

thus hampered in your ability to love, you're being "visited." Instead of blaming the other person for not making you happy, look to see how the idolatry has come in your own life. Within this relationship, what actions or ideas have established a foothold for idolatry?

Although Esau could find no place for repentance, I'm convinced of better things concerning you. The very fact that you're reading this book indicates you're not in the same helpless position Esau was in. If you desperately want a relationship to work out, you'll discover the power to love when you find a place to repent of idolatry and look to Jesus Christ as your source of supply. I hope you'll find His grace in your present situation, and that it will flow in and through you like a flood.

Remember this sixth characteristic of idolatry when you consider your own inability to love.

- **God judges the iniquity of idolatry in the hearts of His people by giving them over to its power. Beware the unwanted "visitor."**
- **God gives us over to the spirit of idolatry in order to reveal its presence and lead us to repentance.**
- **God does this because He is a jealous God.**
- **The spirit of idolatry reproduces itself in our own lives.**
- **The spirit of idolatry reproduces itself in our children's lives.**
- **The spirit of idolatry feeds on a distorted view of God. Pray for God to reveal Himself to you in truth!**

All this could almost seem hopeless if we didn't have the promise of God in the rest of Deuteronomy 5:10-11 as well as in other Scriptures. Although we'll always be walking out a repentance to God for idolatry, we know that Jesus Christ has made sin powerless through His atoning work on the cross. Knowing that our old selves have been crucified with Christ that we should no longer be slaves to sin (Romans 6:6) gives great hope. The blood of Jesus Christ is able to cleanse us from all sin and iniquity.

Let us remember also the verses which follow this commandment in Deuteronomy. Yes, God is a jealous God who judges the iniquity of idolatry, but He promised that He also is…

> …showing lovingkindness to thousands, to those who love Me and keep My commandments. You shall not take the name of the Lord your God in vain, for the Lord will not leave him unpunished who takes His name in vain (Deuteronomy 5:10-11).

To not apply the reality of the death of Jesus Christ for *all* the sins of His people is to take the name of the Lord in vain. Why would anyone take the name of the Lord to himself or herself? Is it not to receive forgiveness and mercy to the glory of God?

Since idolatry is an iniquity which stretches across the generations, you may want to ask God to be merciful not only to yourself, but to those who have gone before you. Much like the Israelites of Ezra's day who confessed the iniquities of their fathers before the Lord, so you also may ask God to break the power of the iniquity of idolatry and forgive you. Ezra prayed,

> O my God, I am ashamed and embarrassed to lift up my face to Thee, my God, for our iniquities have risen above our heads, and our guilt has grown even to the heavens. Since the days of our fathers to this day we have been in great guilt, and on account of our iniquities we, our kings and our priests have been given into the hand of the kings of the lands, to the sword, to captivity, and to plunder and to open shame, as it is this day.

But now for a brief moment grace has been shown from the Lord our God, to leave us an escaped remnant and to give us a peg in His holy place, that our God may enlighten our eyes and grant us a little reviving in our bondage. For we are slaves; yet in our bondage, our God has not forsaken us, but has extended lovingkindness to us… (Ezra 9:6-9).

Hallelujah!

Chapter 10

Hate/Love

Characteristic #7
The spirit of idolatry produces a hate/love relationship.

Deuteronomy 5:9 You shall not worship them or serve them; for I, the Lord your God, am a jealous God, visiting the iniquity of the fathers on the children, and on the third and the fourth generations of *those who hate me,*

Have you ever felt that you loved someone, but at the same time couldn't stand him or her? One wife remarked about her husband, "I love him, but I hate him." She felt she couldn't live without him, but also couldn't live with him!

Such a hate/love relationship signifies an idolatrous relationship. How can someone love God when he or she has sought God only for self-protection, comfort, or temporal blessings? God's children seek Him for protection from evil, relief from pain, and "daily bread"--to name a few. But idolaters never want to say, "If it be your will, Lord, for me to suffer, then give me grace" or "Glorify Yourself, Lord, in my situation." How can a person give to someone with the love of Jesus Christ when he's trying to get something for himself from them? It's impossible. As we discussed in chapter 7, when we expect someone to fulfill our needs, we are actually giving that person the power to make us miserable and hateful.

Hatred for God

It may perhaps be argued that the false gospel that has grown to prevail in the church over the past 175 years has been the greatest stimulus in the hearts of people to hate God. Humanistic influences have distorted the purpose of God and salvation so that churches today present a man-centered, man-glorifying "altar call" from a god who apparently wants to grant our every wish.

What does an idolater think when he hears some of the following invitations to accept Christ? "God loves you and has a wonderful plan for your life." Or "Come to Jesus, and He'll give you the greatest high of your life." Or "If you'll believe in Jesus, He promises to make you healthy, wealthy, and successful." Or "God has a place in His heart which only *you* can fill." Or "If you'll just ask Jesus to come into your heart, He promises to come in and fellowship with you forever." We could probably fill this page with other statements that set up an idolater to hate God. Each of these statements rejects the sovereign God of the Bible in favor of a man-glorifying god who is subject to the free-will decisions of natural men.

Let me explain. I think most people feel a need for God --not the need they ought to feel because of sin, but one which rises out of normal human weakness and emptiness. The Bible teaches that we're born idolaters, users, getters, looking for a life of comfort and happiness-- here and now. Our thoughts about God and what He can do for us don't change until His Spirit changes our hearts.

The prevailing so-called gospel message today appeals to the natural man looking for a user-friendly god. That's the kind of god we all seek until God reveals Himself. I've mentioned before what the apostle Paul wrote about all men, but it bears repeating in this context.

> What then? Are we better than they? Not at all; for we have already charged that both Jews and Greeks are all under sin; as it is written, "There is none righteous, not even one; there is none who understands, there is none who seeks for God; all have turned aside, together they have become useless; there is none who does good, there is not even one. Their throat is an open grave, with their tongues

they keep deceiving, the poison of asps is under their lips; whose mouth is full of cursing and bitterness; their feet are swift to shed blood, destruction and misery are in their paths, and the path of peace have they not known. There is no fear of God before their eyes.

Now we know that whatever the Law says, it speaks to those who are under the Law, that every mouth may be closed, and all the world may become accountable to God; because by the works of the Law no flesh will be justified in His sight; for through the Law comes the knowledge of sin (Romans 3:9-20).

The idolater looks for a god that is compatible with his own thinking--and the "God who is" won't fit that mold. An idolater would never come up with a righteous God who requires what man cannot perform--who says that there's nothing you can do to make yourself right or save yourself. To think of or believe in a God who has chosen a people to be His own from before the foundation of the world is unthinkable to the natural mind. Who of us would ever imagine that a good God would use Satan, darkness, the wicked, and suffering to accomplish His purposes in the lives of His beloved throughout history?

We want a God who loves us and makes us comfortable and happy. Most people have a very difficult time finding any consistency between the realities of life and what they have been taught about God that He loves the whole world, He wants everyone to be saved, He wants to bless His children (He would never hurt anyone), and He is all powerful. Such a God sounds great, and we'd love to have a God like that, but it's not happening. If He loves the whole world and is all powerful, then why does He let bad things happen to good people--especially someone like me? If He wants everyone to be saved, then why doesn't He save everyone? And what about me? If He wants to bless His children and not hurt them, then why do they suffer hardship, persecution, and trouble like--no, more than--everyone else? As one ol' boy from the country once remarked, "That dog won't hunt!"

What is an idolater to think about a God who bears Himself a testimony through martyrdom, persecution, and suffering? And what do we think about a God who promises a life of discipline and reproof?

93

Who, when He determines to heal, first exposes sin and selfishness? Who breaks before He mends? Who crucifies before He raises up?

A young man once came up to a very popular evangelist and charged him with bearing a false gospel. He accused him with something like this: "If you had told me the truth, to come to Jesus and die, I might have made it! But instead, you told me that Jesus would give me the greatest high of my life." The evangelist, in an attempt to lure the young man into making a decision for Christ, had offered a gospel which was not really a gospel. He hadn't told the truth about God or about man. He had implied that God wanted to make him happy and that man had the power to control God through a decision of the will. When the events and relationships in life did not conform to what he'd been told about God, he "fell out of love" with God. His conclusion was that God didn't work. The result was that the man hated God and the evangelist.

A message and method which appeals to the creature comforts and sensualities of man produces a love/hate relationship with God. Its fruit is evident: bondage to the law, pride of man, intolerance, aggressiveness, deceit, hypocrisy, all the deeds of the flesh, confusion, despair, devastation or defection, and NO PEACE.

The truth is that naturally, we hate God because we are idolaters in heart. But that idolatry doesn't only produce a hatred toward God. It also leads to...

Hatred for Others

When we love with the world's kind of love, we seek to get something from others. We say we love them, but in reality, we don't love them at all. Instead, we lust after them. Having to have something from them to be happy, we give them the power in their wills to please us or to frustrate us. Believing that they can, if they choose, make us happy, we tend to hold them responsible for our misery or discomfort. Either their blindness to our need or their sensitivity to pleasing us depends upon what God is doing in them with regards to us. The truth is, the blame rests on us for trying to use them. Our unhappiness or hatred reveals the true motives of our actions and the basis for the relationship.

If we're going to learn to love, we must recognize that hatred for others ultimately comes from a hatred for God. When we grumble or complain about another person we are subconsciously saying we dislike God's providence and sovereign will. We hate what He has chosen for us. If *we* were God, *we* would choose for everyone to treat us with respect and love.

The Lord Jesus told the young lawyer that the greatest commandment is to love God with all our hearts, souls, minds, and strength. He continued and equated loving others with loving God (Matthew 22:35-40). The converse is also true. If we hate our brother, we also hate God. The apostle John wrote, "We love, because He first loved us. If someone says, 'I love God,' and hates his brother, he is a liar; for the one who does not love his brother whom he has seen, cannot love God whom he has not seen" (I John 4:19-20).

We can only love God when He reveals Himself to us. Until then, our god is a god of our own making (or the making of someone who is thinking like we do and who wants us to join his organization). This god must be an idol because it is not the true God revealed in the Bible. When God reveals Himself to His people through Jesus Christ by His Spirit, we have the basis for loving God. If we love God, we recognize that He is our God and the supplier of all things. Obnoxious, stubborn individuals, preoccupied husbands, strong-willed wives, and people unlike ourselves all are sent to us out of the loving intercession of Jesus Christ--for our blessing. The only way we *can* love them is to ask God for the humility and grace to do so. Looking to Christ within us to express love towards them expresses love for God.

Though Jesus hated evil, He never fell prey to hatred toward His Father or others. Even when being persecuted, He asked God to forgive them. When cursed, He blessed. I started to write, "When things didn't go His way," but realized, they always went His way! His way was the Father's way. They were one. Jesus' kind of love bears the characteristics of joy, peace, patience, kindness, goodness, faithfulness, gentleness, self-control; it is not jealous; does not brag and is not arrogant, does not act unbecomingly; it does not seek its own, is not provoked, does not take into account a wrong suffered, does not rejoice in unrighteousness, but rejoices with the truth; bears all things, believes all things, hopes all things, endures all things. His love never fails (Galatians 5:21-22; I Corinthians 13:4-8).

It has been said that if you can be offended, God will keep sending difficult people your way until you are unoffendable. I would like to add that once you're unoffendable, He'll still send difficult people your way who need to be loved with His love. *As the Holy Spirit informs us of the presence of the spirit of idolatry and we look to Him as the source of our life and love, we are equipped and free to love God and others.*

It has helped me to recognize this characteristic of idolatry: *the spirit of idolatry produces a love/hate relationship.* Whenever I feel a twinge of hatred for anything or anyone in my life whom I think I love, I know that the spirit of idolatry is hindering the flow of love in my heart for God and that person. All I have to do is ask Him to reveal the point or issue of idolatry, and He will. Then I ask Him to release His love, thankfulness, and joy in my heart toward them.

Reviewing the Characteristics of the Spirit of Idolatry

- **The spirit of idolatry believes there is more than one god or source of supply for our needs.**
- **The spirit of idolatry attempts to manipulate or control people and situations.**
- **The spirit of idolatry makes an idol for self.**
- **The spirit of idolatry looks to the creature rather than the Creator.**
- **The spirit of idolatry serves many idols.**
- **The spirit of idolatry reproduces itself.**
- **The spirit of idolatry produces the fruit of a hate/ love relationship.**

PART THREE

Equipped To Love

Chapter 11

Repentance and Faith

God Grants Repentance and Faith

> If we had forgotten the name of our God, or extended our
> hands to a strange god, would not God find this out? For
> He knows the secrets of the heart (Psalm 44:20-21).

I n the classic novel by Daniel Defoe, Robinson Crusoe was stranded
alone on a beach with nothing but a Bible to read. After being
greatly convicted of his sin, he fell on his face in the sand and cried out,
"Oh, God! Grant me the gift of repentance!"[1] There could be no more
appropriate response if God has graciously used the previous chapters
to convict you of the sin of idolatry in your relationships with God and
others.

The kind of repentance Robinson Crusoe desired involves a godly
sorrow for sin which entails an understanding of God's hatred for that
sin. We find this kind of repentance described in 2 Corinthians 7:9-11.

> I now rejoice, not that you were made sorrowful, but that
> you were made sorrowful to the point of repentance; for
> you were made sorrowful according to the will of God, in
> order that you might not suffer loss in anything through us.
> For the sorrow that is according to the will of God pro-
> duces a repentance without regret, leading to salvation; but
> the sorrow of the world produces death. For behold what

earnestness this very thing, this godly sorrow, has produced in you: what vindication of yourselves, what indignation, what fear, what longing, what zeal, what avenging of wrong! In everything you demonstrated yourselves to be innocent in the matter.

When God grants repentance (a "sorrow according to the will of God"), deliverance is on the way. Paul wrote that such a repentance leads to salvation. Joseph Alleine, author of *Alleine's Alarm to the Unconverted*, described how one receives such godly sorrow in his counsel to those needing to repent. He suggested that one needs to "labor to get a thorough sight and lively sense and feeling of sins. Till men are weary and heavy laden, and pricked at the heart, and quite sick of sin, they will not come to Christ for cure, nor sincerely enquire, 'What shall we do?' They must see themselves as dead men, before they will come unto Christ that they may live."[2]

In writing to Timothy, Paul gave direction for how the bond-servant of God should correct those who are ensnared by the devil. It is clear that Paul considered repentance a gift and work of God which comes after one is corrected according to God's Word and with gentleness.

And the Lord's bond-servant must not be quarrelsome, but be kind to all, able to teach, patient when wronged, with gentleness correcting those who are in opposition, if perhaps *God may grant them repentance leading to the knowledge of the truth, and they may come to their senses and escape from the snare of the devil, having been held captive by him to do his will* (I Timothy 2:24-26).

As the Lord's bond-servant, I have made this my prayer and a motivating factor as I write and speak the message contained in this book. I've been encouraged by the working of God to bring people to their senses so that they can escape from the snare of the devil who has used the spirit of idolatry to hold people captive to do his will.

If you recognize the sin of idolatry in your heart, now would be the best time to heed Paul's words in 2 Corinthians 13:5, "Test yourselves to see if you are in the faith; examine yourselves! Or do you not recognize this about yourselves, that Jesus Christ is in you-- unless indeed you fail the test?" Are you equipped to love? Is Jesus Christ in you?

May God grant repentance to you! If you have seen clearly the characteristics of the spirit of idolatry in your life, then God's mercy rests on you. *He grants power to repent by giving new eyes by which to see sin.* If you recognize the spirit of idolatry, then it no longer remains in the darkness. If your eyes have been opened to see the truth about idolatry and God's kind of love, then you have reason to hope and believe God is setting you free from Satan's grip. Perhaps now would be a good time to pause and give Him thanks and praise for His goodness and kindness. Ask Him to give you His kind of repentance.

Repentance is Based Upon God's Word

As I encourage you toward repentance, I'm reminded of what Moses said to the people of Israel when He warned them about trusting in idols. They needed to know the seriousness of the sin of idolatry so that they might be convicted and have contrite hearts.

> See now that I, I am He, and there is no god besides Me; It is I who put to death and give life. *I have wounded, and it is I who heal*; and there is no one who can deliver from My hand....*Take to your heart all the words* with which I am warning you today, which *you shall command your sons* to observe carefully, even all the words of this law. *For it is not an idle word for you*; indeed it is your life (Deuteronomy 32:39, 46-47).

The words which are not idle are the words of God. It is His Word which "is living and active and sharper than any two-edged sword, and piercing as far as the division of soul and spirit, of both joints and marrow, and able to *judge the thoughts and intentions of the heart*. And there is no creature hidden from His sight, but all things are open and laid bare to the eyes of Him with whom we have to do" (Hebrews 4:12-13). You can be sure that your idolatry has been evident to God from the beginning of your life. And His Word and Spirit are sufficient to produce a deep work of grace and love, so I would like to turn your attention to some clear, New Testament passages regarding idolatry.

In God's eyes, idolatry equals spiritual adultery. It demonstrates unfaithfulness to one's Creator. As you notice God's attitude toward idolatry may the Holy Spirit speak to your heart.

1 Corinthians 5:9-11 I wrote you in my letter not to associate with immoral people; I did not at all mean with the immoral people of this world, or with the covetous and swindlers, or with idolaters; for then you would have to go out of the world. But actually, I wrote to you not to associate with any *so-called brother* if he should be an immoral person, or covetous, or *an idolater*, or a reviler, or a drunkard, or a swindler--not even to eat with such a one.

1 Corinthians 6:9 Or do you not know that the unrighteous shall not inherit the kingdom of God? Do not be deceived; neither fornicators, *nor idolaters*, nor adulterers, nor effeminate, nor homosexuals,…shall inherit the kingdom of God.

1 Corinthians 10:7, 14 And do not be idolaters, as some of them were; as it is written, "The people sat down to eat and drink, and stood up to play." Therefore, my beloved, *flee from idolatry*.

2 Corinthians 6:16 Or what agreement has the temple of God with idols? For we are the temple of the living God; just as God said, "I will dwell in them and walk among them; And I will be their God, and they shall be My people."

Galatians 5:19-23 Now *the deeds of the flesh are evident*, which are: immorality, impurity, sensuality, *idolatry*, sorcery, enmities, strife, jealousy, outbursts of anger, disputes, dissensions, factions, envying, drunkenness, carousing, and things like these, of which I forewarn you just as I have forewarned you that those who practice such things shall not inherit the kingdom of God. *But the fruit of the Spirit is love*, joy, peace, patience, kindness, goodness, faithfulness, gentleness, self-control; against such things there is no law.

Ephesians 5:5 For this you know with certainty, that no immoral or impure person or covetous man, who is *an idolater*, has an inheritance in the kingdom of Christ and God.

Colossians 3:5 Therefore consider the members of your earthly body as dead to immorality, impurity, passion, evil desire, and greed, which amounts to *idolatry*.

1 Peter 4:3 For the time already past is sufficient for you to have carried out the desire of the Gentiles, having pursued a course of sensuality, lusts, drunkenness, carousels, drinking parties and *abominable idolatries*.

1 John 5:21 Little children, *guard yourselves from idols*.

Revelation 21:8 But for the cowardly and unbelieving and abominable and murderers and immoral persons and sorcerers and *idolaters* and all liars, their part will be in the lake that burns with fire and brimstone, which is the second death.

Revelation 22:15 Outside are the dogs and the sorcerers and the immoral persons and the murderers and *the idolaters*, and everyone who loves and practices lying.

These verses convince us that *those who practice idolatry in their relationship with God and others will not spend eternity with God, regardless of what religious affections and forms they have gone through which appease their consciences.* Those who practice idolatry and who are strangers to a repentance that involves conviction and contrition for idolatry are in for a rude awakening. It is the knowledge of the truth which brings us to our senses and produces a supernatural repentance.

Repentance Involves Conviction and Contrition

When God grants repentance to us in an area of our lives, it is also associated with faith toward God. Repentance and faith are like two sides of a coin. So when we see where we have been wrong, faith toward God leads us to do things which bring about changes. There are a number of things you may do to keep in step with the Holy Spirit as He works genuine repentance. Alleine suggested meditating on the number of your sins, on how your idolatry offends God, on what such harlotry deserves from a holy, just God, and on how this sin has deformed and defiled the image of Christ in you.

As you meditate on these things, God will generate a sincere contrition for your lack of love and for idolizing God and others. *Contrition is a sincere remorse for wrong-doing characterized by humility because of the guilt.*[3] Through making us aware of our own spirit of idolatry, God graciously allows us to sense the guilt we have denied, rationalized through blaming others, and stuffed deep within our souls and bodies.

Why is it so important that you sense the guilt for the idolatry in your life? Isn't that just stirring up unnecessary discomfort if we're already Christians? Perhaps, but maybe not. If in your previous experiences of repentance, God revealed these things to you, then yes, there's no need to stir it up again.

On the other hand, if you've never seen the root of your sin, it may be that you're not yet a Christian! And God intends to save you from the delusion and darkness of "holding to the form but denying the power." I realize this may be a very uncomfortable suggestion, perhaps unthinkable and offensive, but let me explain further why I would suggest such a thing.

Since my wife and I are two who went through the motions of praying a prayer to "accept Christ" at early ages but didn't experience the reality of God's granting repentance and faith until we were both 29, I'm aware of the emotional and spiritual difficulties involved here. But the freedom to love and the peace with God that resulted from sincerely examining our lives and experiences in light of God's clear Word is worth the discomfort! In fact, it explained much confusion and answered many questions I had about myself. I had often wondered how I could be a Christian and do the things I did. When I questioned my salvation before others, I usually was told the devil was tempting me and that I just needed to "drive a stake" and settle it once and for all (ignoring the fact of God's will, power, and purpose for my life).

When I finally realized at age 29 that I had not been given repentance and faith by God Himself because of what He wanted to do in my life and ministry, I could thank God for His wisdom. I then understood why previously I was so powerless, unloving, and selfish. It was like being set free from the snare of the devil who had held me captive to do his will through a lack of knowledge of the truth about God, sin, myself, and God's way of salvation.

A friend of mine, Brian, made this comment: "It took several years of God challenging me along the way to face the ramifications of Scriptures like these [the above] on idolatry. I assumed I was safe--I could consider no other possibility--because I had 'accepted Jesus.'"

Brian also had only gone through the motions of repentance and faith but had never experienced the kind of repentance and faith God grants until he faced his idolatry and its influence on all of his actions. Like Brian, my wife, and myself, you may have suffered the delusion which comes to many who were exposed to an evangelistic method some call "decisionism." This type of evangelism only emphasizes the outward aspects of repentance and doesn't speak about or lead someone to recognize God's work in the heart. Once one thinks he "has it," why would he ever naturally come to a point of questioning sincerely if his faith is genuine?

D.L. Moody believed that repentance and faith consists of five characteristics: conviction, contrition, confession of sin, conversion, and confession of Christ.[4] It is important not to miss any one of the five. Conviction, contrition, and conversion sometimes can be overlooked in our haste to bring a person to a decision for Christ. Many evangelistic presentations only deal with a profession of sin and of faith in Christ.

The groundwork for a God-wrought repentance and faith may take time though. We want to be careful not to lead someone through the motions of a decision for Christ and have them come short of God's gracious work in the heart. If one doesn't *know* his sin, but only knows *about* sin, he may be misled as to his condition and position before God. If the balm is applied before he feels the pain and the guilt, he may not sense the reality of his sin. Consequently, he may experience a lack of love for Jesus and others because he has been converted. His second state is now worse than his first. Like Brian, he thinks he's saved, yet the Scriptures plainly say that no one who practices idolatry will enter into the kingdom of heaven!

But if one is brought to face God and His wrath and to gain a sense of his sin, the wounding of the pride of man will pave the way for true conversion and healing. It puts the soul in touch with reality: his sinfulness and a more realistic understanding of his need for trusting in Jesus' substitutionary death on the cross. But not only that, the man becomes equipped to love!

This is not say that when God implants saving faith in our hearts that we won't ever commit the sin of idolatry again. We will, but it won't be the practice of our lives. Having been enlightened as to the characteristics of the spirit of idolatry and understanding that faith to-ward God is to look to Him as the source of everything in our lives gives us a basis for a continuous repentance of idolatry and love for God and others.

Jesus once was invited to the home of a pharisee named Simon. Simon didn't extend to Jesus the customary courtesies a host should have offered. But a woman of ill repute bravely entered Simon's house, disregarding the scorn and piercing glares, and washed Jesus' feet with her tears and hair. When Jesus received a word of knowledge about Simon's disgust over the woman's actions, Jesus told Simon a parable about two people who were in debt and were forgiven their debts by the moneylender. He then asked Simon this question, "Which of them therefore will love him more?" Simon replied rightly, "I suppose the one whom he forgave more." The Lord summarized his lesson to Simon (and to us) by saying, "For this reason I say to you, her sins, which are many, have been forgiven, for she loved much; but he who is forgiven little, loves little" (Luke 8:40-48).

When God produces repentance and faith, He reveals sin and grants contrition and conversion. Sometimes this takes hours, days, months, or even years--depending upon God's plan. God keeps His promises and glorifies His Son as a heart that He has brought to contrition calls on Him. David wrote, "Behold, Thou dost desire truth in the innermost being, and in the hidden part Thou wilt make me know wisdom" (Psalm 51:6). The Thessalonians showed evidence of God's work in their hearts: "For they themselves report about us what kind of a reception we had with you, and how you turned to God from idols to serve a living and true God, and to wait for His Son from heaven, whom He raised from the dead, that is Jesus, who delivers us from the wrath to come (I Thessalonians 1:9-10).

May God give you a contrite and broken heart regarding this sin of idolatry. But beware the lies of the enemy who may lead you to think idolatry is so great a sin that the Lord Jesus' sacrifice on your behalf is insufficient. It is God's forgiveness of your sinfulness that demonstrates the love of God toward you. When you have the assurance of God's love in Christ in the face of all your idolatry, you'll know that it's time to praise God. I'm sure you'll want to thank God for the forgiveness of sins which comes through your union with Jesus Christ and His shed blood. Praise God for repentance and forgiveness through Christ!

Repentance Involves Confession and Conversion

As you turn to God in faith to serve Him, He'll lead you to turn away from serving the idols in your life. He gives us the Holy Spirit to light the way. So in the light of what we have discussed in the previous chapters regarding a life-style of idolatry, you might ask the Holy Spirit to reveal your "trail of idolatry." As He brings people to mind, I suggest you confess them to someone such as your husband, wife, or parents while confessing them to the Lord. Probably, some of the idolatrous relationships are active relationships at this point in your life.

As God gives you a clear view of how idolatry has been an offense toward God and how it has defiled those relationships you will receive the ability to bless them as you ask their forgiveness for carving on them and rejecting them as God's gift to you. You might ask them to list the carving tools by which they have been most wounded. This will give you further insight into the schemes of the devil, open up more opportunities for grace as you humble yourself before them, help in making restitution, and give God opportunity to perfect His love in you toward them. *This is the fruit and evidence of conversion*!

You may also have confidence that the Lord Jesus wants to take back the "surrendered ground" in your life. I'm speaking with reference to a stronghold as opposed to the principle of indwelling sin. A stronghold of idolatry develops from years of practice. As you idolized God and others, the spirit of idolatry took up residency in a part of your soul. From those places it torments and destroys relationships today.

Here's where the good news of the gospel applies to our lives. Jesus Christ has broken the power of cancelled sin! You may ask boldly for the Lord Jesus to take back the ground given to idolatry. The Lord Jesus has bought the "ground" of your soul with His own blood. That trespassing spirit has been in hiding, undisturbed. But not anymore! If the Lord weren't ready to deliver, He would never have caused its exposure. May the Holy Spirit cleanse every part of your heart and soul that you may love with a holy love.

Loving with a holy love, God's kind of love, lies outside the range of our own natural ability. But God hasn't left us without help or instruction in what we're to do as we confess sin and trust in Christ to forgive and cleanse us of idolatry. We are put on the Lord Jesus Christ if we're to love with God's kind of love.

♦ **God grants repentance and faith toward God.**
♦ **Repentance is based on God's Word.**
♦ **Repentance involves conviction and contrition.**
♦ **Repentance involves confession and conversion.**

Chapter 12

Put on Jesus Christ

I n Colossians 3, the apostle Paul encouraged his readers
to repent of idolatry. Then he gave them clear direction as to what
their next step should be: put on the new self in Christ.

> But now you also, put them all aside: anger, wrath, mal-
> ice, slander, and abusive speech from your mouth. Do not
> lie to one another, since you laid aside the old self with its
> evil practices, and have *put on the new self* who is being
> renewed to a true knowledge according to the image of the
> One who created him--a renewal in which there is no dis-
> tinction between Greek and Jew, circumcised and uncir-
> cumcised, barbarian, Scythian, slave and freeman, *but
> Christ is all, and in all.* [Notice how he recognizes that
> Jesus Christ is to be seen in all of His people.]
> And so, as those who have been chosen of God, holy and
> beloved, put on a heart of compassion, kindness, humility,
> gentleness and patience; bearing with one another, and for-
> giving each other, whoever has a complaint against any-
> one; just as the Lord forgave you, so also should you.
> *And beyond all these things put on love*, which is the per-
> fect bond of unity. And let the peace of Christ rule in your
> hearts, to which indeed you were called in one body; and
> *be thankful*. Let the word of Christ richly dwell within
> you, with all wisdom teaching and admonishing one an-

other with psalms and hymns and spiritual songs, singing
with thankfulness in your hearts to God.

And whatever you do in word or deed, do all in the name
of the Lord Jesus, giving thanks through Him to God the
Father (Colossians 3:8-17).

Now that you have recognized the spirit of idolatry and have been
granted repentance, you can put on love, the perfect bond of unity.
Paul indicated that the basis for putting on love was that we had been
chosen and loved by God. We have God's love for us as an example to
follow. He loved us with an idolatry-free love! Also, knowing the
characteristics of idolatry gives insight into the characteristics of love.

As children of God, we look completely to God, the Father, as the
source of love. Whereas the old self carved and manipulated people
for its own use, the new self seeks to be used to benefit and serve others. We lay down our lives for others by the power of Jesus' life within.
People take on a new purpose. Instead of our estimating their value
based upon what they can give or do for us, we see Jesus' purpose in
all. *The most unattractive individuals are esteemed with greater honor
because in loving them we demonstrate the glorious, selfless love of
Christ who gave his life for those who were unworthy and unlovely.
The more difficult the individual or circumstance, the greater the potential for glorifying our Lord.* That's the perspective of the new self in
Christ.

In the great love chapter in I Corinthians 13, we find that love is
the greatest gift given by God to His people. Of all the gifts we're to
seek, the gift of love should be first and foremost. Without it, we're
playing cymbal solos to those who know us, and we amount to nothing. Consider the qualities Paul wrote concerning love and how they
are impossible while idolizing someone.

Love is patient, love is kind, and is not jealous; love does
not brag and is not arrogant, does not act unbecomingly; it
does not seek its own, is not provoked, does not take into
account a wrong suffered, does not rejoice in
unrighteousness, but rejoices with the truth; bears all things,

believes all things, hopes all things, endures all things. Love
never fails (I Corinthians 13:4-8a).

When I am not seeking to use someone or get anything from them,
I can be *patient* with them because I'm receiving from God exactly
what I need at the moment from them to demonstrate my dependence
upon Jesus Christ. Since I'm not selfishly wanting others to serve me,
I can be *kind* to them. Knowing that God is the supplier of all things,
jealousy has nothing in me to hook. If all things come from God, then
bragging and arrogance don't arise because of gratefulness to God for
His goodness and provision to me. *Love never fails* because I know
that all things come from God and that they have a good purpose of
giving me an opportunity to trust and love.

I can almost hear one who has suffered or is suffering extreme
emotional or physical abuse from someone questioning, "Are you saying that I'm supposed to thank God for this person who is so abusive
and just let him/her beat me up and destroy me and my loved ones?
That can't be loving!" The answer: "Yes, and no."

Yes, I am suggesting that if you are to love with God's kind of
love, you must thank God sincerely for the opportunity He has provided you to demonstrate His kind of love and to experience His love
flowing through you. But, no, I'm not suggesting that the loving thing
is to stay in the situation and continue exposing yourself and your loved
ones to abuse. As you thank God for the opportunity to love, the loving
thing might be to actually remove yourself from the situation temporarily yet remain committed to reconciliation and extend forgiveness.
It is a loving thing to remove a provision of the flesh which gives opportunity to wickedness and destruction. In a sense, if someone is in a
habit of abusing you, your removing yourself is actually in their best
interest.

If you are trusting in God as the One Who is in control of all the
affairs of life, you believe that you have what you need to experience
and demonstrate His love. Also the person's abuse affords you the opportunity to demonstrate your faith toward God and pray from your
position of weakness and pain. This deepens your relationship with
God. Your forgiving the abuser because of the cross of Christ and your
continued commitment to reconciliation glorify the Son of God. Your

not looking to the one abusing you as a supply for love and care frees you to love with God's kind of love.

Paul told Timothy that true believers have been given a spirit of love (2 Timothy 1:7). Having a heart to give to others and be of use to God as a channel of blessing is a wonderful gift from God which comes through the Holy Spirit. We're freed to love for the glory of God when we:

- **Know to distinguish between the world's kind of love and God's kind of love**
- **Understand that love and idolatry are mutually exclusive**
- **Are equipped to discern the characteristics of the spirit of idolatry**
- **Have been granted repentance for the sin of idolatry**
- **Look to God through Jesus Christ for the ability to love**

Perhaps putting on Jesus Christ is still somewhat vague and mystical to you. How does one practically look to God and the Lord Jesus for love? Jesus gave clear direction in His last sermon to His disciples. Perhaps we can pick up some pointers!

Chapter 13

Love Comes From God

H ave you ever considered how Jesus loves His people? As you read the Gospels now, you'll notice how free He was from the spirit of idolatry. He always believed everything came from His Father. Never did He expect anyone to serve Him, love Him, or give to Him. He came only to worship and serve His Father. Because He was filled with the Holy Spirit, a Spirit jealous to love His Father, He loves His people.

Remember the definitions of God's kind of love and the world's kind of love that we looked at in Chapter 2? I'm grateful that Jesus didn't love me with the world's kind of love. I was of no use to Him. Now I find my only significance: as an object of and a channel for the pure love of God in Christ. He loved me, not expecting me to supply anything to Him. He took me in the condition in which the Father gave me to Him: dead in sin and worthy of eternal separation in outer darkness. In seeing His love I'm filled with His love.

He didn't complain when the Father told Him that He must bear my iniquities and griefs. In fact, "He was oppressed and He was afflicted. Yet He did not open His mouth; like a lamb that is led to slaughter and like a sheep that is silent before its shearers, so He did not open His mouth" (Isaiah 53:7).

Why and how could He do that for me? I think it was because He didn't idolize His Father. *He believed and trusted that His Father always gave Him just what He needed to express the Father's glory.* His trust is the exact opposite of the spirit of idolatry.

We see this kind of faith exemplified in Jesus' encounter with Pilate. When Pilate declared to Jesus that he had the authority to release or crucify him, Jesus demonstrated His trust and love for His Father by responding, "You would have no authority over Me, unless it had been given you from above" (John 19:10-11). That's how Jesus faced everything: with an understanding that all came to Him from His Father.

Such an amazing foundational truth provides the basis for an amazing love. An old hymn by Charles Wesley thrills my heart every time I hear it. How about you?

> And can it be that I should gain an interest in the Savior's
> blood?
> Died He for me who caused His pain, for me who Him to
> death pursued.
> Amazing love! how can it be, that Thou my God shouldst
> die for me!
>
> He left His father's throne above, so free, so infinite His
> grace.
> Emptied Himself of all but love, and bled for Adam's help-
> less race.
> 'Tis mercy all, immense and free, for, O, My God, it found
> out me.
> Amazing love! how can it be, that Thou my God shouldst
> die for me!
>
> Long my imprisoned spirit lay fast bound in sin and nature's
> night.
> Thine eye diffused a quick'ning ray; I woke--the dungeon
> flamed with light!
> My chains fell off, my heart was free; I rose, went forth,
> and followed Thee.
> Amazing love! how can it be, that Thou my God shouldst
> die for me!

No condemnation now I dread: Jesus, and all in Him, is
   mine.
Alive in Him, my living Head, and clothed in righteousness divine,
Bold I approach the eternal throne and claim the crown
   through Christ my own.
Amazing love! how can it be, that Thou my God shouldst
   die for me!

Jesus' Last Words

Jesus' love is an idolatry-free love. He doesn't look to us to supply anything, nor does He manipulate us for selfish ambition. It's the
kind of love which comes from His Father. Jesus' last words to His
disciples (recorded in John 14-16) are significant because they are given
within the context of the command to love. His disciples had been told
that He was going to leave them, bodily, but the nagging question was
how they were going to know His presence and His love once He was
with His Father. Jesus' answer gives us insight into how God's love
comes to us and flows through us.

That the Father May Be Glorified in the Son

One of the first things which stands out in Jesus' message is the
motive for all that we do. Jesus' primary interest was, and still is, the
glory of His Father. He promised, "And whatever you ask in My name,
that will I do, *that the Father may be glorified in the Son*" (John 14:13).

The reason God's children long for a relationship with Him is so
their God, Creator, and Father may be glorified in His Son! Those who
have been born of the Holy Spirit pray, love, and obey because they
want the Father to glorify Himself through His Son *in them*. Those
who are born of the spirit of idolatry do the same things but with a
different motive. They pray, love with the world's kind of love, and
obey so they won't go to hell or so God will make them comfortable
and happy.

When God pours out His love on someone, it is really a response
to His Son, Whom He has given to the person, and Who wants to see

115

His Father glorified. God's giving His love isn't a response to a person's praying, serving, and sacrificing for the kingdom. The Lord isn't interested in our sacrifice, but in showing compassion through His Son. The Lord Jesus instructed the Pharisees, who relied upon their outward, religious form and practice, "But go and learn what this means, 'I desire compassion, and not sacrifice,' for I did not come to call the righteous, but sinners" (Matthew 9:13). So, the first thing which should be emphasized here is the motive of the Father to glorify Himself in His Son as He works in and through us.

Jesus Does the Work

The second outstanding point in Jesus' message is His promise to work in His children. The natural man wants to do the work himself because he feels the need to gain the approval of his idol (whether it be a person or a false god of his imagination). But the man born of God's Spirit desires to see Jesus do the work and receive the glory. If you're to be equipped to love with God's kind of love, you must realize the source of that kind of love--God through His Son. That's how God glorifies His Son. Jesus promised that if you will ask the Father to glorify the Son in you, HE WILL DO IT. "And whatever you ask in My name, *that will I do*, that the Father may be glorified in the Son. If you ask Me anything in My name, *I will do it*" (John 14:13-14). Thus, Jesus first shows us His Father's purpose to glorify Himself in His Son in us; and second, He promises to do the work in us when we approach Him with that same desire. But *how* does this practically take place?

When We Abide in Him

We don't often use the word abide in our conversations these days, so perhaps we need to get a grasp of the concept of abiding. When we ask someone where they "live," we are usually asking about their place of residence, the place where they stay. Abiding carries the idea of a home. Jesus began his message saying that He was going to go prepare a place for His people with His Father and that there were many "mansions," "dwelling places," or "abiding places." What's glorious to think about is that there are as many "abiding places" as there are children!

There's a docking place for everyone who trusts in Jesus. God knows we need His presence all the time. We need a home, a place to STAY. And that's exactly what is meant by "abide." It means that we are to constantly stay in this position. We're to live there continually. Where is that home, that place to stay and live? It's with Jesus Christ.

Jesus gave simple directions for how to abide, stay, live, continue, and walk in Him. The first aspect of abiding is...

Pray Always

As you've read the descriptions of the characteristics of idolatry and considered God's kind of love, you perhaps have been bombarded with a sense of hopelessness and neediness. Perhaps you've wondered if you have ever loved or can ever love. That sense of neediness is exactly why we pray. We pray because of our neediness and powerlessness. And it's okay! God intended us to pray always when it comes to loving.

It's wonderful to know that when I am faced with God's righteous commandments or whatever else I read in His Word that reveals His nature and character, it is supposed to also draw me to Him! Awareness that something is right doesn't free me to love. I've found freedom and hope in knowing that I am a weak and empty vessel, knowing my need of Him, and knowing that He desires to reveal His power, His love, and His life--in me!

In chapters 14-16 of the Gospel of John, Jesus spoke often of His commandment to love. But notice how often prayer is mentioned.

> **John 14:13** And *whatever you ask* in My name, that will I do, that the Father may be glorified in the Son.
> **John 14:14** *If you ask* Me anything in My name, I will do it.
> **John 14:16, 20** And I will ask the Father, and He will give you another Helper, that He may be with you forever...In that day you shall know that I am in My Father, and you in Me, and I in you. [In what day? In the day that you pray, Jesus will pray, and then He will send the Holy Spirit to live and love in and through you.]

John 15:7 If you abide in Me, and My words abide in you, *ask* whatever you wish, and it shall be done for you.

John 15:16 You did not choose Me, but I chose you, and appointed you, that you should go and bear fruit, and that your fruit should remain, *that whatever you ask of the Father in My name*, He may give to you.

John 16:23 And in that day you will ask Me no question. Truly, truly, I say to you, *if you shall ask the Father for anything, He will give it to you in My name.*

John 16:24 Until now you have asked for nothing in My name; *ask, and you will receive, that your joy may be made full.*

John 16:26-27 In that day *you will ask in My name*, and I do not say to you that I will request the Father on your behalf [Why? Because you will ask the Father, yourself!]; for the Father Himself loves you, because you have loved Me, and have believed that I came forth from the Father.

If we're to live with Jesus, we must pray always about everything. We do so because we believe in God and believe also in Jesus (John 14:1). The spirit of idolatry would not pray about anything until it wanted something for itself. When we love God, we recognize all things come from Him, so we ask Him to glorify His Son in us in everything. If we talk to Jesus about everything, we find ourselves "at home" with Him, living with Him, and He with us. As we pray, realizing our need and trusting in His faithfulness, He sends us the Holy Spirit to guide us. Then as we listen to Him, we internalize and apply the Word of God.. And that leads us to the second aspect of abiding. Jesus teaches us to…

Eat God's Word Always

When I eat something, I take it into my body and the food is transformed into muscle and tissue. In a sense, it takes on a new identity as it becomes a part of me. In the same way, Jesus taught us to eat God's Word--read, meditate, and fellowship with Him. When we do, we are "coming home" and "abiding" with Jesus Christ.

The purpose of a personal devotion time or "quiet time" isn't to go through the motions so God will give us a good day. That's using it as a positive carving tool (no wonder it doesn't work). In contrast, the goal of time spent in God's Word is fellowship with God, Himself. In a way, every verse of Scripture stored in the mind provides us a place to abide with Jesus. We can embrace every verse and discover the presence of Jesus!

Indelibly impressed in my mind are encounters I had with a man who had been a missionary to Ecuador. Mr. Clark's reputation was legendary. From the time I met him, I couldn't help noticing that almost every time he opened his mouth, he spoke Scripture. Consequently, the presence of God hung around him like the cloud over Mt. Sinai when God met with Moses!

You will notice that the people to whom you are drawn because of the presence of Jesus are also filled with His Word. The more they are filled with His Word in their conversation and life-style, the more they communicate the presence of the living Lord Jesus Christ. Their lives have the sweet fragrant aroma of Life.

Conversely, if I don't keep His commandments, I know that I don't love Him. When God shows me an area of disobedience, I know He's taking me to a deeper level in my relationship with Him and freeing me to love Him. And when I love Him with the love of Jesus, I do keep His Word, and His commandments are not burdensome (I John 5:3).

Again, consider the significance of the frequent references to "keeping" God's Words in John 14-17. The idea of "keeping" isn't only obedience. It involves holding something fast or guarding it well. If we're to abide in Jesus, we must value His Word, both written and communicated to us by His Spirit. And the Word spoken to our hearts by His Spirit will always be verified by the written Word of God.

John 14:15 If you love Me, *you will keep My commandments.*
John 14:21 He who *has My commandments and keeps them,* he it is who loves Me; and he who loves Me shall be loved by My Father, and I will love him, and will disclose Myself to him.

John 14:23   Jesus answered and said to him, "If anyone loves Me, *he will keep My word*; and My Father will love him, and We will come to him, and make Our abode with him."

John 14:24   *He who does not love Me does not keep My words*; and the word which you hear is not Mine, but the Father's who sent Me.

John 14:26   But the Helper, the Holy Spirit, whom the Father will send in My name, *He will teach you all things, and bring to your remembrance all that I said to you.*

John 15:3 *You are already clean because of the word* which I have spoken to you."

John 15:7 If you abide in Me, and *My words abide in you*, ask whatever you wish, and it shall be done for you.

John 15:10 *If you keep My commandments*, you will abide in My love; just as I have kept My Father's commandments, and abide in His love.

John 15:12 *This is My commandment*, that you love one another, just as I have loved you.

John 15:15   No longer do I call you slaves, for the slave does not know what his master is doing; but I have called you friends, *for all things that I have heard from My Father I have made known to you.*

John 16:13-14 But when He, the Spirit of truth, comes, *He will guide you into all the truth*; for He will not speak on His own initiative, but *whatever He hears, He will speak*; and He will disclose to you what is to come. He shall glorify Me; for He shall take of Mine, and shall disclose it to you.

John 16:25   These things I have spoken to you in figurative language; an hour is coming when *I will speak no more to you in figurative language, but will tell you plainly of the Father.*

John 17:6-8   I manifested Thy name to the men whom Thou gavest Me out of the world; Thine they were, and Thou gavest them to Me, and *they have kept Thy word*. Now they have come to know that everything Thou hast given

Me is from Thee; *for the words which Thou gavest Me I have given to them; and they received them*, and truly understood that I came forth from Thee, and they believed that Thou didst send Me.

John 17:14 *I have given them Thy word*; and the world has hated them, because they are not of the world, even as I am not of the world.

John 17:17 Sanctify them in the truth; *Thy word is truth*.

We can have great confidence as we study, memorize, and meditate on God's Word that the Holy Spirit will bring it to mind when we need it to love. How can we know? Can you imagine what the disciples felt when they realized Jesus was going to leave them? How were they going to remember His Words--three years' worth? They hadn't taken notes. They didn't have computer files or transcripts of his sermons. They were fearful that they would never be able to remember everything. They had counted on His setting up the kingdom in their lifetime.

When we consider that the gospels weren't written until the second half of the first century, fifteen to twenty years after Jesus' death and resurrection, these words of Jesus are astounding: "But the Helper, the Holy Spirit, whom the Father will send in My name, He will teach you all things, and bring to your remembrance all that I said to you" (John 14:26). They were able, by the ministry of the Holy Spirit, to remember conversations, events, and sermons word for word with one hundred percent accuracy! The Holy Spirit can bring the Word of God to your remembrance if you eat His Word regularly. You'll have many "abiding places" as you walk through life.

But is it enough to just gather knowledge and pray? A third aspect of abiding in Christ is necessary if we're to love. Jesus taught us to …

Obey Because of Love

Abiding in Christ also involves love. We obey because He loves us, and we obey because we love Him. As you read the previous verses, surely you couldn't help seeing how often Jesus mentioned obedience because of love.

> **John 14:15** If you *love Me*, you will keep My commandments.
> **John 14:21** He who has My commandments and keeps them, *he it is who loves Me*; and he who loves Me shall be loved by My Father, and I will love him, and will disclose Myself to him.
> **John 14:23** Jesus answered and said to him, "*If anyone loves Me*, he will keep My word; and My Father will love him, and We will come to him, and make Our abode with him."
> **John 14:24** He *who does not love Me does not keep My words*; and the word which you hear is not Mine, but the Father's who sent Me.
> **John 15:9** Just as the Father has loved Me, I have also loved you; abide in My love."
> **John 15:10** If you keep My commandments, you will abide in My love; just as I have kept My Father's commandments, and abide in His love.
> **John 15:12** This is My commandment, that you love one another, just as I have loved you.
> **John 15:14** You are My friends, if you do what I command you.
> **John 15:17** This I command you, that you love one another.

As we obey Jesus' Words, we expect *Him to do it* by the power of the Holy Spirit. When we pray, asking the Father to glorify the Son in us as we love with His love, the Lord Jesus prays and asks the Father to send the Holy Spirit to "help us." Our responsibility is to eat His Word, pray, and obey. When we step out to love as we're commanded, the Lord Jesus prays and promises *to do it*. As we love, Jesus loves. As Jesus loves through us, we abide in His love and know Him personally.

"Beloved, let us love one another, for love is from God; and everyone who loves is born of God and knows God" (I John 4:7). We know God as He loves through us. That's the only way people are going to see God. In John's first epistle, he continued on, "No one has beheld God at any time; if we love one another, God abides in us, and His love is perfected in us" (I John 4:12). *Until God's love flows through Jesus, through us, and to others, His love hasn't completed its course or been perfected. It can't be perfected except through us!*

A phrase made popular through an evangelistic campaign in the 1970's was "God loves you and has a wonderful plan for your life." The kind of love presented by that phrase is the kind of love any idolater would want. It's a love based upon what God does for *you* and is often associated with good feelings about God and one's feeling that he's gained God's approval. God's love was seen in His sending His Son to die for *your* sins. And since He loves *you* so much, you now ought to return that love and give yourself to God and love others. Unfortunately, the focus of this idea is not so much God revealing His purpose and His love as it is on me, on my getting things, having a "wonderful" life, and feeling cared for.

Although there are some wonderful truths sprinkled throughout such a presentation, it misses the Biblical idea of God's love. According to John, one can't say he's been loved by God until that love is perfected in him. *Until love has completed its course and traveled from God through His Son, through the believer to another undeserving soul, one cannot know that he's loved by God.* "God loves you," sounds great, but there's more to it than your feeling cared for.

The apostle John continued in the fourth chapter, "And we have come to know and have believed *the love which God has for us*. God is love, and the one who abides in love abides in God, and God abides in him. There is no fear in love; but *perfect love casts out fear*, because fear involves punishment, and the one who fears is not perfected in love. *We love, because He first loved us.* If someone says, 'I love God,' and hates his brother, he is a liar; for the one who does not love his brother whom he has seen, cannot love God whom he has not seen" (I John 4:16, 18-20).

When God loves through us, *we see God and His Son*. We discover the truth that Jesus is in the Father, and the Father is in Jesus, and we are in Him, and He is in us (John 14:20). Only "perfect love" casts out the fear of judgment. He isn't referring to the world's kind of love which produces warm fuzzies in His children, but God's kind of love which has completed its course and blessed others. As I love someone in obedience to Christ and pray that the Son will glorify the Father in me, the Holy Spirit manifests the presence of Christ in me to the person I'm loving. At that point, God's love is perfected in me, but not in my brother. When my brother whom I've loved, loves out of a relationship with Jesus Christ, God's love is then perfected in him. To God be the glory!

That's the love of God we must teach in our evangelism and discipleship. Let's take the world's kind of love out of our thinking and be witnesses to a love that comes from God. *You can be equipped to love.*

- ♦ **We are loved by God when He loves through us.**
- ♦ **Our motive is that God be glorified in the Son.**
- ♦ **Jesus works in us as we abide in Him through prayer, eating His Word and obeying out of love for Jesus.**

Your being equipped is entirely dependent upon Jesus' ability, not your own; for remember His words, "Apart from Me you can do nothing" (John 15:5). By abiding in Jesus, you can love. And that's the opposite of idolatry.

Chapter 14

Generations Equipped to Love

Deuteronomy 5:10 But showing lovingkindness to thousands, to those who love Me and keep My commandments.

As I talk with believers of my generation, I find that most have a heart to see their children trained and prepared for marriage and parenting. They don't want their children entering adulthood encumbered with the emotional and sensual baggage with which they entered those years. For many of us, we're still throwing off habits and appetites acquired during the 60's and 70's when we were playing instead of preparing. We're just now learning what's important as we suffer the reproofs of selfish living. We want something better for the next generation!

I hope you feel that way. We have a hope, not in our abilities, but in Him who has promised to show His lovingkindness to thousands, to those who love Him and keep His Word. *God wants to make a difference in generations.*

What a blessing we can give to our grandchildren if we envelop our children in God's kind of love and lead them to its Source! Our sons and daughters will not have to go through the destruction in relationships if they abide in Christ and learn how to love while they're young. I'm very excited about this because I've witnessed it firsthand. In the past two years, our daughters, Abby and Alyssa, have married. They and their husbands know more about how to love than we knew when we were 35. They not only have knowledge of facts, but they know *Who* love comes from and how to walk with Him. And their children will be blessed even further than that because they plan to love with God's kind of love and teach their children early about idolatry and from Whom love comes. I think God intended the family to be the laboratory where people learn how to love.

Love Needs to Start With the Men

Love needs to start with us men. Consider the burden of a wife and children who must live under the authority of one who does not know how to love. Fathers and husbands, how much of your relationship with your wives and children has been based on your use of them for your own comfort, convenience, and pleasure? You single men, when you think of getting married, do you primarily think of getting your own needs met? If you're like me, I didn't have a vision for anything but those things when I began my married life! Although I'm very grateful to my parents for having taught me to care for and serve others, I didn't know how to do it without the influence of the spirit of idolatry until I became aware of the characteristics of that spirit.

As a father loves his wife, his daughters are powerfully influenced to either reject or accept their design as women. If a daughter sees her dad use her mom, she probably will develop a negative attitude toward womanhood and marriage. On the other hand, if a daughter sees her father love her mother with the love of Christ--protecting, serving, honoring, listening, understanding, and gently guiding her--she will likely embrace her womanhood and marriage with joy and expectation of good things. What impact are you making on your daughter?

Your son will probably also model your husbanding and fathering. He will love his wife as he sees you love your wife (or his mother). From you he'll discover what it is to love a woman. (If he doesn't learn God's way from you, he'll learn the world's way.) You'll influence generations to come if you'll include your son in creatively loving your wife. Teach him how to love his sisters and mother with God's kind of love. How he loves them will probably be the foundation for how he loves his wife. Dad, you are the leader! What is your son learning about loving women from you?

Most important of all, your wife and children need to learn how to love God. In Deuteronomy 6, God put the responsibility on the fathers to train the children in their relationship to God. We see it repeated in Ephesians 6 by the apostle Paul. If our children are to come to a saving knowledge of God, they must come face to face with their idolatry.

God has called us men to be the spiritual leaders of our families and to be "sound in faith and love," as Paul wrote to Titus. We're not only to exemplify love to our families, but we're to teach them *how* to do it--through repenting of idolatry and through a relationship with Jesus Christ. As channels of God's Word to our families, all the verses on idolatry need to be presented, taught, and brought to bear on their consciences. Then they can come to know their need for abiding in Christ.

Our children also need to have a vision for training their children with these things. My prayer is that God has used this book to equip you to love your wife and children with the love of Jesus Christ, and that the fruit of it will be seen in many generations to come. Their testimony may be of a dad who loved God and them with God's kind of love. How about you? If you know Jesus Christ, YOU ARE EQUIPPED TO LOVE!

Wives and Mothers

Wives and mothers, have you become aware of the carving tools you've used on your husband and children? I hope so. May God give you grace to love your husband and train your children in the art of loving others. Since you spend the most time with the children, you are in a significant place of influence. Will your daughters know how to love their husbands because they have had you as an example and teacher? Will your son look for a wife who has the same gentle, loving qualities as his mother?

I also want to encourage you who feel your husbands do not yet know how to love. Their weaknesses and inabilities are God's invitations to deeper fellowship with Him. As you go to Him, He may perfect or complete the love of Christ in you for your husband. May God give you the humility, gentleness, wisdom, and boldness to speak in love when God prompts you. You have a tremendous privilege of demonstrating the love of Christ on a daily basis, which may impact many generations to come. If you know Jesus Christ, YOU ARE EQUIPPED TO LOVE!

Children and Teens

I hope there are some children and teens who are reading these words. Some of the best responses I've had to this message have come from some your age. They've been so grateful to learn how to love their parents and siblings and build God-glorifying friendships. As you apply these things to your family, classmates, or friends, you will be preparing for the future. In fact, as you learn how to love your parents, brothers, and sisters, you are practicing skills which will prepare you to be a godly mate and parent. And that influences generations to come! There's no one you can't love with the love of God. If you know Jesus Christ, YOU ARE EQUIPPED TO LOVE!

About to Be Married?

There's probably no more motivated group of people to learn about love than those who are seriously thinking about marriage. Perhaps you picked up this book because you wanted to know how to love before you got married. When I asked my daughter what was the most helpful counsel I gave her before marriage, without hesitation she responded, "It's the knowledge about idolatry and love. Not a day goes by that I don't think about idolatry and look to the Lord for grace to love."

One young man told me that these things were the most important part of his and his wife's preparation for marriage. He said he applies it every day. I pray that God has given you the same blessing as you seek to build your marriage on God's kind of love.

There may be some readers who are considering marriage for the second or third time. I realize what I'm about to say isn't popular and probably won't be received without some serious prayer, meditation, and study. Therefore, I don't expect you to jump up and down and celebrate discovering this truth's application. But, if your previous marriage(s) failed due to idolatry and a lack of love, if reconciliation is possible (your ex hasn't remarried), then it is God's will that you remain committed and love your first husband/wife.

I encourage you to think through the Scriptures on divorce and marriage from the frame of reference of the love you've read about in this book. The idea that divorcing and remarrying is justifiable because of specific sins isn't supported by God's kind of love as described in the Bible. Those interpretations fall under the category of the world's kind of love. But God's kind of love rests on His power and can heal broken marriages.

If you've understood what you've read, you now know why your previous marriage failed. There's no reason to believe that God can't glorify Himself in His Son in you as you seek to reconcile with your former spouse and now love as you should have loved in the first place. You may say, "But my former spouse doesn't know how to love! And I don't feel anything for him/her."

When you put aside what "self" wants (happiness and comfort) and see that your ex-spouse was God's provision for you to demonstrate His love and forgiveness, you'll see that your former spouse's inability to love is exactly what you need now to experience God's love and glorify Him.

If there are children involved, then they also need to see God's kind of love in you! Their lives will forever be changed if they have a living testimony of God's love before their eyes. Generations will be affected by your faithfulness and love. As far as it depends on you, I encourage you to apply these things to your former marriage rather than look for another idol to worship, serve, and carve upon. May God glorify Himself as you seek to love in this way. No one caught up in the world's kind of love can do it. Only someone who is equipped to love with God's love can. And if you know Jesus Christ, YOU ARE EQUIPPED TO LOVE!

Let's Pray

Since love comes only from God, it seems appropriate that we close our time together in prayer. Will you join me?

Our heavenly Father, we are humbled by our sin and inability to love. In the spirit of the prophet Isaiah we cry out to You, for all of us have become like one who is unclean, and all our righteous deeds are like a filthy garment; and all of us wither like a leaf, and our iniquities, like the wind, take us away, and Thou hast delivered us into the power of our iniquities. But now, O Lord, Thou art our Father. We are the clay, and Thou our Potter; and all of us are the work of Thy hand. Do not be angry beyond measure, O Lord, neither remember iniquity forever. Behold, look now, all of us are Thy people. Thy holy assemblies have become a wilderness, Zion has become a wilderness like the world. Wilt Thou restrain Thyself at these things, O Lord? Wilt Thou keep silent and afflict us beyond measure?

We recognize You as the source of all things. Thank You for the circumstances and the people You have wisely given to humble us in order that You might give grace through Jesus. Father, be merciful to us and to our children. Turn our hearts, that we might love them and train them to love also. Raise up this next generation to be bright lights in a dark world.

We cannot fathom the depths of Your love, but we want to grow in love, that we might better understand the dimensions of Your love. Teach us how to love until we reach the maturity demonstrated in Your Son, Jesus Christ. Fill us with His Spirit; that we might love the most unlovely in Your name. Heal relationships damaged by the spirit of idolatry. Remove bitterness and hurt from disappointments and expectations which were based on idolatry. Most of all, set us free to love You with all our hearts, souls, minds, and strength and to love our near ones--in Jesus' name. Amen.

NOTES

Chapter 1. Which Kind of Love?

[1]Oswald Chambers, *My Utmost for His Highest* (Ulrichville, OH: Barbour and Company, Inc., 1963), p. 261.

Chapter 2. Are You Idolizing Others?

[1] *The Philadelphia Confession of Faith* (Sterling, Virginia: Grace Abounding Ministries, Inc, 1981), p. 13.

Chapter 6. More on Carving

[1] James Adams, *Decisional Regeneration* (Pensacola, Florida: Chapel Library), p. 2
[2] Ibid., p. 4
[3] Ibid., p. 5
[4] Iain Murray, *The Forgotten Spurgeon* (London: 1966), p. 110.
[5] C.H. Spurgeon, *The New Park Street Pulpit* (London, 1964), Vol. 6, p. 171.
[6] James Adams, *Decisional Regeneration,* p. 7

Chapter 11. Repentance and Faith

[1]Daniel Defoe, *Robinson Crusoe* (New York, NY: Macmillan Publishing Company, 1983), p. 126.
[2] Joseph Alleine, *Alleine's Alarm* (Carlisle, Pennsylvania: The Banner of Truth Trust, 1978), p. 101.
[3]Ibid, p. 102.
[4] D.L. Moody, *The Overcoming Life* (Chicago, IL: Moody Bible Institute, 1896), pp 31-45.